LAURA WADE
PLAYS ONE

Laura Wade

PLAYS ONE

Colder Than Here

Other Hands

Breathing Corpses

Introduction by Aleks Sierz

OBERON BOOKS
LONDON

WWW.OBERONBOOKS.COM

First published in this collection 2012 by Oberon Books Ltd
521 Caledonian Road, London N7 9RH
Tel: +44 (0) 20 7607 3637 / Fax: +44 (0) 20 7607 3629
e-mail: info@oberonbooks.com
www.oberonbooks.com

Reprinted in 2014, 2017

A catalogue record for this book is available from the British Library.

PB ISBN: 978-1-84943-223-8
E ISBN: 978-1-84943-682-3

Cover image by thomasadank

Printed and bound by 4EDGE Ltd, Hockley, Essex, UK

Contents

Introduction

The theatre critic sets off in the evening to review a new play. It's by a young playwright that he has never heard of before. He's impressed by the play's dialogue; he's convinced by the characterisation; and he is interested in the story. He gives the play a positive review. Then, a couple of weeks later, he has to review another play by the same playwright. But, guess what, it's written in a completely different way. What to do? He looks at the press releases and compares the themes of both plays. Ah yes, that's it. He seizes on the most obvious similarity: both of them are about death. He hails the new playwright as a contemporary chronicler of our attitudes to death. Then, about a year later, the playwright's third play arrives on stage: and it's not about death at all. Time to reassess his first impressions.

With only pardonable exaggeration, this describes the reception of two of Laura Wade's plays in February 2005, and the impact of her third a year later. Since then, of course, she has become chiefly known because of the phenomenal success of her 2010 Royal Court play, *Posh*, which transferred to the West End in 2012. Yet magnificent as that play is, it is worth stressing that her earlier work, although on a smaller canvas, is equally fascinating and equally contemporary. The first play in this collection, *Colder Than Here*, opened at the Soho Theatre in London in February 2005. By then, Wade was a graduate of the Royal Court's Young Writers Programme and had already had a success on the fringe with *Young Emma* – her adaptation of the memoir by W H Davies – at the Finborough. In fact, she'd been writing plays since the age of seventeen for the Crucible Theatre in her hometown of Sheffield, and then for Playbox Theatre at Warwick, and for Bristol University and the Bristol Old Vic. *Colder Than Here* was written while Wade was on the Royal Court's Young Writers Programme, and the idea came from an article she'd read about green burials, an ecologically friendly way of treating the deceased. It's a strikingly original idea, and she researched woodland burial sites while inventing her characters.

The core situation of the play is that Myra, a fiftysomething woman, is suffering from terminal bone cancer, and Wade developed a family situation in which the necessity for getting on with life rubs up against the reality of rapidly approaching death. The resulting tension produces humour and stoicism. Myra's family is composed of her husband Alec, who is pretty buttoned up, and their two daughters, the older Harriet and the younger Jenna. There's a neat contrast between the highly organised Harriet and the more confused Jenna. Over the course of the play, the scenes alternate between the parental home and visits to burial sites, one of which Myra must choose as her final resting place. This is a normal middle-class family in the sense that there are no great violent outbursts, no exaggerated rhetoric, although each of them is on a distinct emotional journey. There's also something very English about the Leamington Spa setting and the gentle air of melancholy which suffuses the work.

What is immediately striking in the play is not only the mature grasp of family relationships, especially those between mother and daughter, and between female siblings, but also the impressive economy of the writing. The storytelling has a wonderful lightness of touch, yet at the same time a very strong thematic coherence and metaphorical resonance. The theme of death, for example, is pointed up by small details, such as when Myra says that Jenna learnt to smoke in a graveyard, a thought which leads like a wisp of smoke to the idea of cremation, and to its rejection in favour of a woodland burial. As the play's title indicates, the overarching metaphor is the sense of the coldness of death, which is grounded in a feeling that the emotional atmosphere in the family is quite chilly. The coolness of their relationships is emphasised by the fact that the boiler in the household has broken down, and that daily life is lived in a damp chilliness, which feels like a symbolic preparation for the grave. Even the electric heater proves impossible to fix. At the same time, each member of the family is on a path towards a better emotional state, and while at first communication between them is mediated by discussions about the cat, or, in one unforgettable scene, via Myra's Powerpoint presentation of her ideas for her own funeral, by the end of the play each person has found the ability to talk openly about their feelings.

The notion of having in some way to rehearse their bereavement provides an emotional thread that runs through the play. Jenna, the daughter who is a bit of a drama queen, both acts out her unhappiness and withholds herself from her mother. Gradually, she opens up. By contrast, Harriet, who starts off as well-organised and capable, ends up feeling totally confused, which she expresses by using the recognisably apt metaphor of carrying washing upstairs, when 'one sock falls off the top of the pile and I bend down to pick it up but while I'm doing that something else falls'. In the end, even the coldness of Alec and Myra's marriage enjoys a moment of sunshine. In the original production, directed by Abigail Morris, Michael Pennington's Alec gently kissed Margot Leicester's Myra on the forehead. A beautiful touch. Equally engaging was the contrast between Georgia Mackenzie's Harriet and Anna Madeley's Jenna, both of whose body language showed how family relationships were gradually thawing.

But good dialogue exists not just to make stage relationships convincing, nor just to convey information, but also to entertain the audience. There are plenty of eccentric moments in *Colder Than Here*, like the game about objects whose appearance we are unfamiliar with. At the same time, the play also lightly touches on several taboo subjects apart from death, such as that of talking to your parents about your sex life, and on stage there are several memorable images, chief of which is when Myra tries out her ecologically friendly cardboard coffin. The coffin seems like a child's improvised craft, now ready to take you on one final voyage. By the end of the play, not only does the moss at the burial site feel warm, suggesting a thaw in the freeze between Jenna and Harriet, but also the family is talking about talking, a good start in their belated quest in search of communication. Dying is a tough subject. In *Look Back in Anger*, John Osborne's Jimmy calls it a 'sordid process', and it's kept offstage. By contrast, *Colder Than Here* is more honest and humane in unflinchingly showing the way that people face the inevitable, with humour, with silence, sometimes clumsily, sometimes stoically, and ultimately with love.

If one of the problems facing new playwrights is the expectation that each of their plays should be similar in style,

Wade's next play, *Breathing Corpses* proved that you could radically change both form and content. While *Colder Than Here* portrayed a familiar world of women, *Breathing Corpses* presented a frieze of unusual situations, unusual jobs and unusual characters. All of which are linked by the theme of acute personal unhappiness. First staged in the Royal Court Theatre Upstairs, also in February 2005, the playtext had an epigraph from Sophocles: 'When a man has lost all happiness, he's not alive. Call him a breathing corpse.' For while *Colder Than Here* is a play about waiting for death, in chilling anticipation of the loss of a loved one, *Breathing Corpses* is about accidentally discovering the dead bodies of strangers. As each of the characters find a murdered body or the result of a suicide, they experience the physical reality of death and decomposition. Here the scene in *Colder Than Here* in which decomposition is discussed becomes a ghastly reality. This a play in which the smells, touch and feel of death is unavoidable. At one point, a character comments on the expected response to death, how you have to 'feel the length of it', meaning how long it might affect your life. Finding a body makes you suddenly super-self-aware of details, like the 'dirt up my fingernails'. The sight of a corpse becomes imprinted on the retina. Something indelible. Like the 'unconnected flashes of horror' that 1960s child killer Mary Bell – in Gitta Sereny's book *Cries Unheard* – remembers when picturing her crimes. Added to these intensely lived sensations are metaphorical associations, such as the smelly dog food and the story of the stored doner kebab meat that goes off and spawns a maggot invasion.

Wade invents three storylines: that of nineteen-year-old Amy, a chambermaid in a mid-price hotel, of fortysomething Jim and Elaine, who run a self-storage facility, and of Ben and Kate, a couple where the woman is older, more successful and more dominating. Each of the characters Amy, Jim and Kate find a body, and each also becomes a body that is found by one of the other victims. The drama has a thrillingly non-linear form, where the story of how the discovery of one corpse leads to another is told by using a structure in which some scenes are chronological and some not, a device which creates a sense of dislocation that emphasises the inability of the characters to communicate. So

Amy finds a corpse on two occasions while cleaning a hotel room. It turns out that the second corpse is that of Jim, whose depression has worsened after he himself found the corpse of a woman in a box at work. And that dead body turns out to be a woman killed after a quarrel with her boyfriend, during which it emerges that she – in a 'surreal' turn of events – found a corpse in the park while walking his dog Cameron. Because of the play's fragmented structure, the full story of such spooky coincidences only fully emerges in the final scene.

Watching the play on stage was an exciting experience, and Anna Mackmin's cracking original production included Laura Elphinstone (Amy), Paul Copley (Jim), Niamh Cusack (Elaine), Tamsin Outhwaite (Kate) and James McAvoy (Ben). All the coincidences made perfect sense. The last scene mirrors the first, and you left the theatre, your brain buzzing with all the connections between the living and the dead, the happy and the unhappy, the corpses and their discoverers. Arriving home, there was a real temptation to grab a sheet of paper and go through the playtext, mapping out the scenes, listing how they relate to each other. Doing this inevitably reveals the secret of the play's plotting, the fact that it tells an impossible story in the same way that a print by M C Escher shows an impossible building. And it's also perfectly circular, with the ending looping back to remind you of the beginning like a bizarre hall of mirrors. It's the kind of play that makes you imagine a parallel universe in which the scenes repeat into infinity. It's a testament to the power of the writing that *Breathing Corpses* can give you such crazy ideas.

If the writing in Wade's *Colder Than Here* was aptly polite, here it throws off all restraint, and becomes as dangerous as piranhas and as noisy as barking dogs. But although the dialogues are speeded up, as if a shot of adrenaline has been injected into them, this is still a play firmly rooted in character. Amy is so lonely that she chats to the corpse she discovers and foolishly, but entirely credibly, becomes fatally drawn to Charlie in the last scene. Jim, the kind of man who bothers to correct apostrophes, is unable to articulate his depression in any healing way. Despite the efforts of Elaine to help him communicate, he is in a very strange place indeed, and his account of little black fish swimming into his eyes is disturbingly weird. Yet his helplessness in the face of death is instantly recognisable, and the plight of this couple – whose sons have left home and don't stay long when they visit for Christmas – is both common and sad. Likewise, the relationship between the vicious Kate and the longsuffering Ben is a study of unhappiness in which the woman is both the main breadwinner and the main abuser. It's a power relationship that feels both truthful and appalling. And if gender roles are not always predictable, there is no denying the solitude of the characters. Elaine wants Jim to talk to her, but he can't; Ben does talk to Kate, but she won't listen; and no one ever notices Amy. To adapt the words of Tolstoy, all happy people resemble one another, each unhappy person is sad in their own way.

The central themes of loneliness and difficulties with communication continue into the third play in this collection, *Other Hands*, which was first performed at the Soho Theatre in February 2006. Having been together for eight years, computer geek Steve and management consultant Hayley barely speak to each other. Non-communication has become a habit. 'Everything I say feels like I've said it before,' she complains, while he remains stuck to his PlayStation. In their early thirties, their life paths have diverged. And things have changed: Hayley is now the main breadwinner; Steve has gone freelance, and earns very little. Worse, the unresolved tensions in their relationship manifest themselves in a painful affliction of their hands. As in *Breathing Corpses*, there is an atmosphere of sensuality, and of its disturbance. Hands help us to feel, to do things, to touch loved ones. Painful hands disable us; make us vulnerable, impotent. From the prehistoric cave paintings of hands at, for example, El Castillo in Spain, to the dozens of metaphorical expressions in which we give someone a hand or hand on knowledge, they are a symbol of our humanity.

Equally human is our frustration with those closest to us. With quirky humour and a loving attention to detail, Wade shows how both Steve and Hayley drift towards strangers, their clients: Steve gets interested in Lydia; Hayley flirts with Greg. In one of the most erotic scenes in contemporary British drama, Greg and Hayley describe having sex with each other, in a purely verbal game of desire which takes place in a coffee bar. But although this sexy encounter leads Hayley to realise that: 'Oh my god the grass isn't just greener I mean it's got ten-foot sunflowers I can I can *smell* them', it also confirms her feeling that she can't have an affair. In the end, neither Steve nor Hayley is unfaithful, and his conclusion – 'I just think we've got to be braver' – applies to both of them. Bijan Sheibani's meticulous original production, with Anna Maxwell Martin (Hayley), Richard Harrington (Steve), Katherine Parkinson (Lydia) and Michael Gould (Greg), brought out Wade's characteristic mix of brutality and tenderness, leaving you at the end with the feeling that this particular couple had just pulled back from the abyss.

It is a play rooted in vulnerabilities. Being dependant on technology leads to helplessness when the machines break down. The contrast between having the technology to be in touch globally, but being unable to talk to those nearest to us is an insight shared by most critics of contemporary urban life. As Albert Einstein said in a different context, 'It has become appallingly obvious that our technology has exceeded our humanity.' Here vulnerability is akin to unhappiness. The image of a woman welcoming a stranger, especially a man, into her home is also one of vulnerability, exposure to danger. In the coffee bar sex scene, the disarming need for connection is expressed sexually, but it is also a negotiation about terminology which might characterise the start of an intimate relationship. Above all, psychological problems manifest themselves physically: both Steve and Hayley have trouble with their hands. But the pain is ambiguous: are they suffering from Repetitive Strain Injury or Carpal Tunnel Syndrome, or rheumatoid arthritis, or just a psychosomatic paralysis? Whichever it is, they are alienated from their own bodies, from their selves.

For textual trainspotters, there are some anticipations of troublesome or symbolic hands in Wade's previous plays: in *Colder Than Here*, Harriet's eczema on the back of her hands is clearly psychological in origin and in the first scene of *Breathing Corpses* Amy holds the corpse's hand in her lap, saying 'Cold hands' and noticing the liver spots on its skin. Sadly she is trying to make a connection with a person who is long gone. As in

Other Hands, unhappiness is manifest by physical distress. Steve and Hayley desperately need to talk, but they don't really know how, so her provocative Scene Three curtain line – 'I want to sleep with someone else' – is taken literally by him. It should be an opener to further discussion, but instead it slams shut a door. Only when the play comes full circle at the end can the desperate cry behind this act of bravado be heard. Only then do they learn to talk.

Other Hands has a quartet of deftly drawn, if not always very likable, characters in a drama where the women tend to be quite quirky and the men emotionally semi-literate. Hayley might be efficient, but she also feels baffled; Lydia is helpless, but has great potential. Both Steve and Greg are on a search for a braver life. There's an appealing tentativeness in these people. Wade's touch is marvellously light and beautifully observant, while the writing avoids sentimentality and has a strongly metaphorical undertow. The comparison between the human body and the world of mechanical technology suggests ideas about emotional healing and technological repair, while the problems in both areas seem invisible, hidden by darkness – behind malfunctioning screens or in the unconscious – and needing expert attention. At the same time, the modern corporation is also seen as an ailing beast that requires fixing by management consultants like Hayley. In this context, she acts like a machine, rationalising the business by sacking human beings. If numbness is the human response to repetition, whether at work or in the home, kindness is the answer. In this play, with a wonderful sense of fitness, the victim of workplace rationalisation helps the victims of emotional distress to travel up the long road to self-knowledge. At the end, in the touching final scene, there's a real sense of healing. Individuals can learn to change, and take their lives into their own hands.

In 2005, Wade won the Pearson Best Play Award for *Breathing Corpses*, and was joint-winner of the George Devine Award. She also won the Critic Circle's award for Most Promising Playwright. Not every writer delivers on their early promise. As this collection clearly shows, Wade certainly has.

Aleks Sierz, London, September 2012

COLDER THAN HERE

For Michael

My thanks to the following for their love, support or help with *Colder Than Here* (in some cases all three): Michael Shaw, Charlotte Mann, Rod Hall, Tamara Harvey, Jack Thorne, Jamie Carmichael, Tina and Stuart Wade, Heather and David Shaw, Celia Harvey, Simon Stephens, Nina Lyndon and all at the Royal Court Young Writers Programme, Vicky Jones, Neil McPherson and Emily McGill. And, of course, Abigail Morris, Nina Steiger and all at Soho Theatre.

Characters – a family

MYRA
aged 56

ALEC
aged 57

HARRIET
aged 29

JENNA
aged 27

SETTING

The action moves between the living room of the Bradley
family home in Leamington Spa, and various woodland /
greenfield burial sites around the West Midlands.

Colder Than Here was first performed at Soho Theatre on 3 February 2005, with the following cast:

MYRA, Margot Leicester
ALEC, Michael Pennington
HARRIET, Georgia Mackenzie
JENNA, Anna Madeley

Director Abigail Morris
Assistant Director James Hammond
Designer Naomi Wilkinson
Assistant Designer Polly Webb-Wilson
Lighting Designer Nigel Edwards
Sound Designer John Leonard

*A burial ground in the West Midlands. Midday. Mid-September –
almost autumn but still warm enough not to wear a coat or carry an
umbrella.*

*The site is young, the trees just a few years old and still spindly. There are
no headstones – graves are marked by shrubs or trees with the occasional
wooden plaque.*

*MYRA stands looking around her. She is noticeably thin but surprisingly
energetic. She is suffering from advanced secondary bone cancer, but
today has little pain.*

*JENNA, her daughter, aged 27, stands a little way off, a large picnic
basket beside her. She wears mostly black, with a long stripy scarf.*

MYRA: Here.

JENNA: Here?

MYRA: Yes, I think so. Don't you think so?

JENNA: I'm not– I don't know.

MYRA: I think here is good. Flattest bit. Under a tree– I like
that, nice and shady. Let's say here.

MYRA indicates an area on the ground.

JENNA: Fine.

MYRA looks at JENNA. JENNA doesn't move.

MYRA: Yes?

JENNA: Fine.

JENNA looks around.

MYRA: Bring the basket over.

JENNA: You want to eat here?

MYRA: Yes.

JENNA: You want to eat. Here.

MYRA: Yes, let's eat, you'll eat here lots. It's out of the sun, it's…

JENNA: It's *morbid.*

MYRA: It's happening, Jen, come on.

JENNA brings the picnic basket over.

MYRA opens the basket and pulls out a large blanket, which she starts to shake out. JENNA looks away.

JENNA: Did you see the. Did you see the baby?

MYRA: No.

JENNA: There's a baby. Under some holly, a holly bush.

MYRA: That's lovely. Never dies, that's lovely.

MYRA is struggling with the blanket.

Could you, um?

JENNA: Yeh.

They lay out the blanket together.

MYRA: Was there a marker?

JENNA: Two months old.

MYRA: Can't say that's a good innings, can you?

MYRA sits down and starts unpacking the picnic.

Now. Plates… Are you warm enough?

JENNA: Fine.

MYRA pulls out two plastic plates. She hands one to JENNA. JENNA holds it like it smells bad.

MYRA: Um, forks…

Hands a plastic fork to JENNA.

Napkins…

Hands a napkin to JENNA.

JENNA: Mum, I don't need a–

MYRA: Have a napkin.

JENNA: I don't want a / napkin

MYRA: Have a napkin.

JENNA takes it.

JENNA: Serviette.

A look.

Basket smells funny.

MYRA: Found it in the cellar.

JENNA looks at MYRA.

I wiped it, it's fine. Everything's in plastic it'll taste fine.

MYRA looks into the basket.

I brought things you like.

JENNA: I don't want anything.

MYRA: Sausage rolls, I've got sandwiches, posh crisps, Jaffa Cakes, quiche, you might turn your nose up at / that–

JENNA: Bloody hell, mum, this lot don't eat anymore, you know.

MYRA: You're picky. Lots of / options.

JENNA: You're not supposed to be cooking and–

MYRA starts to pull food out of the hamper.

MYRA: I didn't. Marks. Jaffa Cakes might be a bit own-brand. Lots of sandwiches.

JENNA: I don't like sandwiches.

MYRA: You don't– Since when?

JENNA: I woke up one morning and realised I'd been living a lie all my life.

MYRA: Oh for God's / sake.

JENNA: I'm bored of them. They're always soggy, people put too much stuff in them, they're impossible to eat.

MYRA: Sausage roll?

JENNA raises her eyebrows.

Vegetarian sausage roll.

JENNA: Not a sausage roll, then, is it?

JENNA takes a sausage roll and starts to pick at it.

MYRA: Know what I hate about sandwiches? When people say the D. SANDwiches.

JENNA: SANDwiches. Samwidge.

MYRA: Exactly. Not SANDwich.

JENNA looks around her, eating her sausage roll.

There isn't one.

JENNA: One what?

MYRA: Toilet. You're looking for a toilet to go to after you eat that.

JENNA: I'm not. (*A look.*) I don't. Mum, I don't.

MYRA: How would I know?

JENNA: I don't do that anymore.

MYRA opens a sandwich and starts to eat it.

There is one, anyway.

MYRA: Jen–

JENNA: What? Just a point of information – there's one by the caretaker's house. I happened to see it on the way in.

MYRA: You were looking.

JENNA: No, I just– we were driving in and I saw it and I though 'oh, a toilet, you need a toilet, all the old biddies that come here'. It's not a toilet I want to yak into.

MYRA looks intently at JENNA.

It's a habit, isn't it? You get used to all the little– things you do kindof around the main thing, even when you stop doing the thing you still have the little– Habits.

MYRA: So eat that properly.

JENNA stuffs the whole sausage roll into her mouth and looks at MYRA, challenging. Swallowing takes longer than she expects and she turns away, breaking the look.

JENNA: That was next-*level* disgusting.

MYRA: Another one? The sandwiches aren't bad, not soggy / really.

JENNA: Every time I see you do I have to stuff my face just to / prove I'm–

MYRA: I got some houmous ones.

JENNA: Fine.

MYRA: Do you like it?

JENNA: Houmous?

MYRA: Here. Do you think we should bury me here.

25

JENNA: I don't want to bury you anywhere.

MYRA: That was almost affectionate.

JENNA: I don't like–

MYRA: It's just that we haven't got long.

JENNA: How long?

MYRA: Six months or so. Up to about nine.

JENNA: Jesus.

Beat.

Does it– Does it hurt?

MYRA: Just aches and pains. I've started to make a noise when I bend down to pick things up.

JENNA: Like what?

MYRA: Kind of 'Uhh'. 'Uhh'. Like an old lady.

Beat. JENNA fumbles in her bag and takes out her cigarettes.

Mind you, your dad does that already, I might just have picked it up off– So you're smoking in front of your mother now?

JENNA: Won't have a chance soon, will I?

MYRA: You giving up?

A look. JENNA puts the cigarettes away.

You learned to smoke in a graveyard, didn't you? You and that boy from the comprehensive–

JENNA looks at her.

What, you think we didn't– You came home covered in lichen, smelling of mints and Impulse. Of course we knew about it. Why I asked you to come, prior knowledge.

26

Haven't told your dad yet. We always said cremation but now it– Think he might find it a bit odd. Cardboard coffin, no headstone or–

JENNA: Cardboard?

MYRA: Or wicker, you can get wicker ones.

JENNA looks at the picnic basket.

Yes, alright. Cardboard ones come flatpack. Self-assembly. You could help.

JENNA: You're kidding, right?

MYRA: No.

JENNA: That's fucked up. Next-*level* fucked up, I'm not doing that.

MYRA: Have a think about it.

JENNA: (*Under her breath.*) Fucked up.

Pause. MYRA eats a sandwich.

MYRA: Maybe plant a holly bush.

JENNA: Does Harriet know?

MYRA: No.

JENNA: Sounds like one of hers.

MYRA: I read a book. You have to find things to do. When you're off work with dying. Leamington Library's got loads of death books, shelves and shelves of cancer. And then this one saying you can be buried somewhere pretty if you want to. Hadn't even thought about it…

Harri had nothing to do with it. I wanted to tell you.

JENNA: Tell her everything else first.

Beat.

MYRA: You had a lot to deal with / at the time.

JENNA: Like what?

MYRA: You'd just got together with Mark. You were– Busy.

JENNA: You'd been to three appointments before anyone said anything.

MYRA: We didn't want to worry you. You worry.

JENNA: It was important and I missed it. 'Hello love, just had my thyroid gland whipped out, how's the new boyfriend?'

MYRA: Does it matter, Jen? Does it really matter. Now.

Pause.

JENNA: Can I have a Jaffa Cake, please?

MYRA hands her the packet. JENNA stands up and walks around, the packet of Jaffa Cakes in her hand. She eats one.

MYRA: Rowan tree, maybe?

JENNA: Ugh, squishy berries.

MYRA: Cherry. Flowering cherry. Just blossom, nothing squishy.

JENNA: Palm tree, get some fucking monkeys…

MYRA: How are they?

JENNA: All right. Chocolate's a bit baggy.

JENNA looks out at the traditional cemetery over the fence.

Why do they have the lawny bit there and then this bit here?

MYRA: Give you a choice?

JENNA: So ugly, all laid out in straight rows, shiny marble, plastic fucking buckets. Someone should go round and take the dead flowers off, looks a fucking mess.

MYRA: This bit's nicer.

JENNA: Have to walk through the plastic buckets to get to you, though.

MYRA: Perhaps you could tell your dad about it, the burial thing. You could tell him for me.

JENNA: Oh mum, I–

MYRA: I mean there may come a time when you two need to learn to talk to each other…

JENNA: We talk.

MYRA: Not really.

JENNA: We get on fine, we don't argue.

MYRA: No, it's a shame.

Give you a reason to come round and see us. Haven't seen you properly in months, when did you last sit and chat to him?

JENNA eats another Jaffa Cake.

JENNA: Dad doesn't like me.

MYRA: Of course he likes you, he loves you.

JENNA: He doesn't *like* me.

MYRA: He doesn't like Mark very much.

JENNA: Yeah, well.

He didn't mean to be rude he's just– That's Mark, I don't know.

Don't think I like him much right now.

JENNA continues to eat Jaffa Cakes as she talks.

Wants to quit work and do a university course 'cause he says it's too much of a strain working in the same shop every day 'cause we end up spending so much time together, which is stupid it's not like we live together is it, but if I won't leave then he'll have to or we'll end up splitting up. Which I think is going to happen anyway 'cause he's flirting with the manager every day and when I question it he says I'm paranoid or possessive or– And he's just. Being a wanker. And–

MYRA: And?

JENNA: Oh, you know. Love him. Twat.

MYRA: How's the sex?

JENNA: What?

MYRA: How is it?

JENNA: The / sex?

MYRA: Yes.

JENNA: I don't– I'm not talking about that with you, we don't talk about that.

MYRA: Maybe we should.

JENNA: Why?

MYRA: I've never managed to get to the bottom of this relationship you're so disastrously having, and we've. We've never had a talk.

It's important / isn't it?

JENNA: Mum, I don't want to–

MYRA: Isn't it?

Beat.

JENNA: You and daddy don't have sex.

MYRA: How do you know?

JENNA: You've slept in separate rooms for years.

MYRA: You've moved out, how do you know what goes on?

JENNA: So what, you're at it all over the house usually, are you? Then when me and Harri come home you move back into separate bedrooms just to keep us feeling secure in the pair of you not fancying each other...

Beat. MYRA looks at her watch.

MYRA: Tablet time. Would you pass the bottle?

JENNA takes a bottle of water from the picnic basket and passes it to MYRA. She watches MYRA take a bottle of tablets out of her bag, put one in her mouth and swallow it down with a drink of water.

JENNA: Sorry.

JENNA puts the Jaffa Cakes back in the basket.

MYRA: While I'm still here I can help. After I kick it you're on your own.

MYRA coughs and drinks more water. JENNA watches her.

Ugh, too big these ones. What?

JENNA: Nothing.

I. Sorry.

JENNA looks around her.

MYRA: So we're happy with here, yes?

JENNA: Sure.

Beat.

Actually, no. I think it's a bit–

MYRA: Yes.

JENNA: I think we could find somewhere. Better.

MYRA smiles.

Fade.

SCENE 2

The living room of MYRA's family home. Mid-evening, late October.

A sofa and an armchair that have been in the same place for many years, newspapers and books in a pile by the armchair. MYRA sits on the sofa, working at a laptop on the coffee table in front of her. She wears warm clothes and has a large glass of white wine next to her. There is a half-finished bottle of wine and a couple more glasses.

MYRA's daughter HARRIET is standing behind the sofa taking her coat off.

MYRA: How was it?

HARRIET: Good. It was good. Dad got cross 'cause someone clapped after the second movement.

MYRA: Were they shot?

HARRIET: Social death. Exclusion from the Brahms fan club… (*Pointing at the wine glass.*) Should you be–

MYRA: Yes. Emphatically yes. (*A look.*) Shut up. Where's Dad?

HARRIET: Loo. What's this?

MYRA: PowerPoint. You going to stay for a drink?

HARRIET: Yes, short one, Josh'll be waiting up. Why you doing PowerPoint?

MYRA gets a glass and pours wine for HARRIET. She uses both hands to lift the bottle.

MYRA: Had it sat on the desktop for years, didn't even know what it was. Thought I'd give it a go now I'm never going to work again…

I'm bored, Harri.

MYRA laughs.

Feel like going back.

HARRIET: Get better first, yeah?

MYRA looks at HARRIET. HARRIET looks away.

MYRA: I'm making a presentation.

HARRIET: Show me.

ALEC comes in, polishing his glasses with a lens cloth. He has already taken his coat off.

MYRA: Next time. Not ready yet. (*To ALEC.*) How was it?

ALEC: The cellist was awful.

HARRIET: Dad she wasn't / awful.

ALEC: She was awful.

HARRIET: Her dress was awful. (*To MYRA.*) Big turquoise mermaidy thing. Looked like a burglar's dog.

MYRA: Drink, Alec?

ALEC looks at the wine.

ALEC: Yes. Just get some red.

ALEC goes into the kitchen to fetch red wine.

MYRA: But nice father-daughter evening?

HARRIET: Yes. And we bought tickets for next time.

MYRA smiles.

Mahler.

MYRA: That's brave.

ALEC comes back with a bottle of red wine and a glass.

HARRIET: Now is it me or is it cold in here?

MYRA: Boiler's on the blink. What?

HARRIET is looking at ALEC, smiling.

HARRIET: We were playing 'phrases Dad hates'.

ALEC: 'Is it me or is it cold in here.' Completely moronic.

HARRIET: What was the other / one?

ALEC: Can't remember.

HARRIET thinks.

HARRIET: 'À propos of'.

ALEC: Well that's just stupid, isn't it? – the 'of' is implied in the 'à propos', it's *there.* Some chump in the interval, shouting his mouth off...

MYRA: You shouldn't see people dear, it makes you cross.

HARRIET: What's wrong with the boiler?

ALEC: Not boiling anything.

ALEC picks up a newspaper and opens it, obscuring his face.

MYRA: Sore point.

HARRIET: Any news on Baggins?

MYRA: Gone for good, I think.

HARRIET: Have you told her?

MYRA shakes her head, drinks some wine.

ALEC: (*From behind the newspaper.*) Sore point.

MYRA: Speaking of sore, we've got another hot spot from the scan last week.

HARRIET: Where?

MYRA points to her left upper arm.

MYRA: Humerus. Great name for a bone. So that's four places.

HARRIET: I'm sorry, mum.

MYRA: Alright, feeling quite sanguine today.

ALEC: Pff.

HARRIET looks at ALEC, then at MYRA.

MYRA: I gave the boiler a good kick this morning…

HARRIET: Sorry I couldn't come with you. I wanted to come to all of them.

MYRA: Turns out you get extra cloying sympathy if you go on your own.

HARRIET: I hope you were nice. They're professionals.

MYRA: Anyway, a couple more places and we'll be able to say I'm riddled with it.

HARRIET: What are they going to do?

MYRA: More radio. Painkillers. Warm baths. Funeral planning.

HARRIET: Don't be– Mum–

MYRA raises her eyebrows. Drinks. HARRIET looks over at ALEC, who is immobile behind his newspaper.

Dad.

ALEC: Yes.

HARRIET: Mum's dying and you're sitting there reading the paper.

ALEC: Watched pot never boils, love.

MYRA laughs, nearly chokes on her wine.

HARRIET: Dad!

MYRA: I like that.

HARRIET: Honestly.

MYRA: It's easier if you find the / funny, believe me.

The front door opens, offstage.

JENNA: (*Off.*) Hello.

MYRA, ALEC and HARRIET look at each other.

JENNA comes into the living room, a large sports bag slung over her shoulder. She stands just inside the door, hesitant.

Hi.

MYRA, ALEC and HARRIET all look at her. JENNA swings the bag onto the floor.

What?

MYRA: Is everything alright?

JENNA: I, um. Thought I might. Stay for a bit. If that's– If that's OK.

MYRA: Have you and Mark had an argument?

JENNA: No. No more than usual. It's all fine, he's fine.

MYRA, ALEC and HARRIET continue to stare at JENNA.

What? Is this. Is this not alright?

MYRA: Of course it's–

JENNA: All looking at me like it's–

MYRA: It's lovely to see you.

JENNA puts her hands in her pockets.

Glass of wine?

JENNA: If it's not too much tr–

MYRA: White or red?

JENNA looks at ALEC's glass.

JENNA: Red.

MYRA goes to pick up the bottle and HARRIET stops her.

HARRIET: Here, let me.

JENNA watches HARRIET. Then MYRA.

MYRA: Harri and Dad went to the concert tonight.

HARRIET pours a glass of wine for JENNA and hands it to her. ALEC goes back to his paper.

JENNA: Was it good?

HARRIET: / Yeah.

ALEC: No.

JENNA: What was it?

HARRIET: The Brahms double.

JENNA: I like Brahms.

HARRIET: Since when?

JENNA: Hungarian Dances – I like that. The one Dad likes.

MYRA: Brahms!

MYRA types something into the laptop.

ALEC: What are you doing?

MYRA: Hungarian Dances, brilliant. Upbeat. You should take Jenna to a concert sometime.

MYRA continues to type.

JENNA: That would be– Um, yeah.

The others are watching MYRA. JENNA pulls her sleeves over her wrists. She moves a little closer to MYRA.

Fucking cold in here.

HARRIET: Boiler's packed up.

JENNA: Oh.

HARRIET: Still want to stay?

JENNA: Course. Yeah.

JENNA drinks some wine. HARRIET watches her from the sofa. ALEC reads and MYRA types.

I'll go put my bag–

JENNA goes to leave with her bag. She doubles back and hugs MYRA over the back of the sofa, then leaves rapidly. The others look at each other.

HARRIET: God knows. D'you think they've–

MYRA: What, split up?

ALEC takes his shoes off.

ALEC: Entrance wasn't dramatic enough.

HARRIET: (*To MYRA.*) She'll tell you.

JENNA returns and stands by the door.

JENNA: Ummm…

ALEC: Ah, the ominous um.

ALEC takes his slippers from beside the chair and puts them on. He puts shoe-trees in the shoes he has taken off.

JENNA: Um, where's Baggins?

ALEC: Ah.

ALEC looks at MYRA.

JENNA: What?

MYRA: Baggins isn't here.

JENNA: God, he didn't get run over again, did he?

MYRA puts her hands together in her lap.

MYRA: No.

JENNA: What, is he– Has he gone on holiday?

HARRIET: Sort of.

JENNA: What?

MYRA motions to HARRIET to fill up her wine glass.

MYRA: He's um. He's moved out.

JENNA: How– How can he have– He's a cat.

MYRA: They're autonomous, love. It's up to them.

JENNA: He's been here fifteen years, this is his home.

ALEC: Went off with another woman.

JENNA looks at MYRA.

MYRA: Alec. He disappeared. Few weeks ago. So I. I put a
card in the newsagents with his picture, the phone number
and. And the next day a lady rang from Kenilworth Road
and said she'd– Got him. She'd been looking after him,
thought he was a stray.

JENNA: He's got a collar.

MYRA: Lost it. She wasn't to know.

JENNA: Fucking cat thief.

ALEC: Cat burglar.

MYRA: Alec. She'd only just moved here and her cat died. I felt sorry for her.

JENNA: You left him there?

ALEC: Course she didn't.

MYRA: We went to get him, with the basket. Kept him inside a few days so he'd readjust and it was fine. Then, how long was it?

ALEC: A week. Thereabouts.

MYRA: Went off again.

JENNA: But you went– You went and got him again?

MYRA: Yes. And the time after that. By the fourth time I thought. Well I thought maybe he, he likes it there. Maybe. So I said–

JENNA: What?

MYRA: I said she could keep him.

JENNA: He's my cat.

MYRA taps her fingernails on her wine glass. JENNA wraps her arms around herself.

HARRIET: You weren't the one looking after him, Jen.

JENNA: Fuck off being fucking reasonable. I'd have taken him if he'd– If I'd been allowed pets in my flat– we can't all afford to buy our own flat, it's not my fault.

MYRA: We had to let him go.

ALEC: Like the lion in *Born Free*.

MYRA: Alec. If he didn't want to be with us…

JENNA: Did you change the brand of cat food?

MYRA looks at ALEC.

Did you?

MYRA: No. No.

JENNA goes out to the kitchen.

ALEC: My fault.

MYRA: It's not.

HARRIET: It's no-one's fault.

JENNA returns, a can of cat food in her hand.

JENNA: He doesn't like this sort. He's never liked this sort. Last time we got this he tried to throw himself under a lorry.

HARRIET: That was completely / disconnected.

JENNA: He doesn't like this.

MYRA: I'm sorry. Your Dad's been doing the shopping. I haven't been. Up to it…

JENNA bites her lip.

I should have told him which sort to get.

Pause.

He might be– Baggins might be better off there, anyway. He's used to having people around, and once I'm– There'll just be your dad here and…

Long pause.

JENNA: (*Under her breath.*) Fuck.

HARRIET looks at JENNA.

What?

HARRIET looks away, pours more wine. Another long pause. No eye contact: four people alone.

MYRA drinks, then stands up.

MYRA: OK, let's do it now.

HARRIET: What?

MYRA: Shall we look at my presentation?

HARRIET: You said it wasn't ready.

MYRA: It's not really, but since we're all together – doesn't happen much, does it? Family time.

ALEC: What's this?

MYRA: Can you come and sit over here between your daughters, please?

ALEC: Not taking a photograph, are you?

HARRIET: Mum's made a PowerPoint thing.

JENNA: A what?

MYRA: Alec, come and sit over here.

ALEC: I'm reading the– (*A look.*) Alright.

ALEC stands up and sits down gingerly between the two daughters on the sofa.

What are we looking at?

MYRA: The computer.

ALEC: Need my glasses.

He's left them on his armchair. He stands up and fetches them.

MYRA: Can't you just–

ALEC: Just a second…

ALEC sits back down on the sofa.

Right.

MYRA: Jenna, you'll have to be my techno person, alright?

JENNA: I don't usually use a–

MYRA: You just have to hit return when I say, OK?

JENNA: OK.

HARRIET: D'you know which return is?

JENNA: Not a fucking / clue.

MYRA: Oh, for God's sake, how can you not– / Even I know–

HARRIET: That one.

JENNA: Thanks.

MYRA: OK, are we ready?

The others nod in assent.

So this is something I've made to. Talk to you about something that– Well, it speaks for itself really. But it's a first draft so– OK. Jenna?

JENNA: Yes?

MYRA: OK?

JENNA: Oh right.

JENNA presses return. She turns to MYRA.

Is that what you're going to say? When I have to press it.

MYRA: I'll say 'Jenna'.

JENNA: OK.

JENNA turns back to the screen, which ALEC and HARRIET are looking at, aghast. The words 'MY FUNERAL, by MYRA

BRADLEY' have appeared. The slides also appear on the back wall, behind the family.

ALEC looks at MYRA.

ALEC: Myra–

MYRA: So I've been thinking about this and how I want to shuffle off. And. I think it's important for you to know. So you don't get it wrong. So we can plan. OK, Jenna.

MYRA smiles at ALEC. JENNA hits return.

ALEC: I don't–

MYRA: So if you could just listen. Watch.

> *ALEC looks back at the screen. The words 'No funeral director or mortician' slide onto the screen from the right. With a swooshing noise.*

> You can make it do all sorts of things – moving and noises and–

> So I want us to arrange it. Not a man in a tailcoat.

> *A Clip Art picture has appeared beside the caption.*

JENNA: Is that a bridegroom?

MYRA: There isn't a funeral director, I told you it's a first draft.

ALEC: You can't do it without an undertaker, it's not legal / is it?

MYRA: It is. There's a guidebook, handbook thing. Death certificates, it's all there. Jenna.

> *JENNA hits return. The caption 'Woodland burial' slides on from the left. A tree appears with a twinkling sound.*

> I'd like to be buried in a–

ALEC: Buried?

MYRA: Yes.

ALEC: Not cremated.

MYRA: No.

ALEC: But we've always– I mean it's, it's in the wills–

MYRA: I'm rewriting mine.

JENNA: It's, um. Cremation's bad. For the environment. It's a
pollutant.

ALEC looks at JENNA.

MYRA: So I want to be buried in a woodland or a nice field.
Jenna and I went to see one last month. Jenna's going to be
head of the burial site committee, help me find somewhere
just right so–

HARRIET: Jenna is?

MYRA: Yes.

We'll need suggestions for a tree to plant on top of me, that
would be helpful. Most of these places you can't have a
marker.

Jenna.

*JENNA hits return. The caption 'Cardboard Coffin' appears on the
screen with a fanfare.*

Beat.

ALEC: Cardboard?

MYRA: They're very strong. Much cheaper.

ALEC: Not the point.

MYRA: They come flatpack – we could order it ahead of time.
You can paint them. I'd like to paint it.

ALEC goes to speak, but can't.

Jenna.

JENNA hits return. The caption 'I will paint. Pillows & plastic liner.' slides down from the top of the screen.

OK, we've talked about that already. Next one, Jen. I haven't put noises on this bit yet...

JENNA hits return. 'Bury me in warm clothes.' appears, sliding down from the top again, followed by 'Velvet scarf. My big red shawl.'

I'm thinking it might be cold down there. Jenna.

JENNA hits return. 'Coffin to be carried by family.' appears from the lower part of the screen.

Perhaps not you, Alec, not with your back.

ALEC takes his glasses off and puts them on the table. He leans back. HARRIET drinks her wine.

It's all a bit sketchy here – just ideas I threw down. Jenna, just page through them.

JENNA hits return at short intervals and we see the following appear: 'Springtime flowers – depends on how long I last.'

So I guess we won't know about that for a while...

The next caption: 'No throwing flowers'.

Looks a bit shoddy, doesn't it? Sounds funny, flowers thudding on the...

Then, next to 'no throwing flowers' appears ' – throw something else.', then, a moment later 'Glitter?'

OK, so that's a bit silly. There should be something like confetti we could use.

ALEC shifts in his seat.

The next caption: 'No Astroturf.' followed shortly by 'For god's sake.'

HARRIET: Astroturf?

MYRA: You know at funerals when they cover up the earth by the side of the grave with fake grass? Like being buried in a greengrocer's.

Jenna, next one?

JENNA hits return. The caption 'Watch grave being filled.' appears.

ALEC: What the–

MYRA: I think you should all stay there and watch while they fill it up.

ALEC: Oh, this is– No, excuse me.

ALEC stands up, moves away from the sofa.

MYRA: I don't want everybody strolling away, leaving me…

JENNA: I feel sick. Feel a bit sick.

HARRIET: You knew about this?

JENNA: Not all of it.

ALEC: We're not going to– This is too–

MYRA: What, love, what?

ALEC: We're not–

MYRA: It's my funeral.

ALEC: Funny.

MYRA: Why can't I make jokes about it, isn't that how we–

Pause.

Please, Alec, we have to–

ALEC: We're not. We're not burying you in a. Cardboard box.

ALEC leaves.

MYRA: Alec. It doesn't go away if we don't–

The others are silent for a moment.

JENNA: Left his glasses. Have to come back down.

They look at the glasses.

HARRIET: Could take them up.

I can't believe you knew about this, why didn't you–

JENNA: I don't know, I–

HARRIET: You just don't *think*, do you?

HARRIET picks up ALEC's glasses and follows him out. MYRA stares at the coffee table. JENNA looks after HARRIET and ALEC.

MYRA: I want it decorated with the sky and the stars.

Fade.

SCENE 3

Another burial ground near Leamington. This is a level meadow with wild flowers and long grasses during the summer, but now, on a wintry Saturday in mid-November, looks a little bleak.

HARRIET and JENNA stand facing each other by a wooden stile. HARRIET holds her lunch – couscous salad in a Tupperware box – which she will continue to eat in a moment.

HARRIET: What, she didn't tell you?

JENNA: What?

HARRIET: She's feeling a bit– Um, yeah.

JENNA: Bit what?

HARRIET: Bit cancerous.

Asked if I'd come instead.

JENNA: She was fine when I left this morning.

HARRIET: Maybe she–

JENNA: Well that's a fat lot of bloody good, isn't it, we're not burying you.

HARRIET: She didn't want to leave you stranded. And your mobile's switched off.

JENNA forages for her phone in her handbag, and eventually pulls it out.

JENNA: Fuck. Always forget to frigging– Forget to fucking lock it…

HARRIET: Anyway, nice to see you, thanks for coming.

JENNA: Thanks.

They look out across the field.

HARRIET: Not up to much, is it?

JENNA: No.

HARRIET: D'you pick this?

JENNA: It's in the book.

HARRIET: Hmm.

HARRIET eats.

God, my boyfriend's a good cook. We were just having lunch, put some in a box for me, bless him. D'you want some?

JENNA: No thanks.

HARRIET: 'S really good.

JENNA: Hate the smell of Tupperware. This family. Always eating in fucking cemeteries.

HARRIET eats, JENNA surveys the field.

Did you hear it arrived yesterday?

HARRIET: Did it?

JENNA: Great big flatpack thing. Postman made some funny about enormous packages, not being able to get it through the letter box...

HARRIET: Who answered the door?

JENNA: Dad.

HARRIET: Great.

JENNA: Then there's a hoo-haa about where to put it. Dad said it should go in the cellar then Mum says it'd get too damp. So then Dad wanders off muttering it'll get a lot damper once it's used...

HARRIET: Where is it now?

JENNA: Behind the sofa. Wants to build it straight away, try it out for size. So we can all get used to it. Apparently if we see it around the place we won't be so upset when she's in it.

HARRIET: Just start sleeping in it, freak us out properly...

Beat. They look around.

Well, I'm glad we didn't drag her all this way, are you?

JENNA goes to sit on the lower bench of the stile.

I mean, how would we know where she was? You'll get a wet arse.

JENNA: Don't care.

HARRIET: It's a bit damp.

HARRIET looks in her rucksack and pulls out a carrier bag.

D'you want a bag?

JENNA: No thanks.

HARRIET spreads out the plastic bag on the upper step of the stile and sits down.

HARRIET: You wouldn't know, would you? You'd have to remember, there's no markers or anything. 'Less they buried her right by the wall. Can't say I like the idea of having to find my mother with a map and a compass.

Beat.

JENNA: Do you miss her?

HARRIET: Do I miss her?

JENNA: Like when people say 'missing you already' when they're saying goodbye. I miss her already.

HARRIET: Thought I'd wait till she's gone, myself.

JENNA takes her cigarettes from her pocket and lights one.

Oh please not here.

JENNA: These places. Give me a death wish.

HARRIET: Do you have to?

JENNA: Yes, I'm addicted. That's what addiction is.

HARRIET: Don't blow it on my lunch. How many have you had today?

JENNA: Umpteen.

Beat.

I miss her. Like the other day, I got home from work and it was a shit day and– I. Wanted her there. And I got home and. Just gripped by it. Desperately wanted her. Lying in bed, crying my eyes out and there's no-one else, no-one else is good enough.

HARRIET stops eating. She looks across the field, away from JENNA, frowning.

Kind of frightening, getting this 'I want my mummy'. Hadn't felt that for years, I mean when did you last feel that, your whole body?

HARRIET: I. I can't remember.

JENNA: So *basic*, like the cord or something, being pulled out from– (*Mimes a cord coming out of her stomach.*) Yeah.

HARRIET: What did you do?

JENNA: Can't cry all day, can you, you run out. Packed a bag and went round to mum's.

HARRIET: Have you told her?

JENNA: Course not. But now I keep thinking about next time I feel like… You ever get days when just breathing too deeply makes you cry?

Beat.

HARRIET: How long are you planning to stay? At home.

JENNA: Don't know.

HARRIET: Cause it seems you've pretty much moved back in.

JENNA: Plenty of time for living in a shit flat on my own when she's–

HARRIET: Don't you think– Don't you think maybe they need some time. Just them?

JENNA stands up.

JENNA: I have got a wet arse now.

HARRIET: Don't you think?

JENNA: She'd ask.

HARRIET: Come on, she couldn't ask that.

JENNA: Why not?

HARRIET: Because you'd react like you always do.

JENNA: Like / what?

HARRIET: Like everything's your tragedy and no one / else's.

JENNA: I don't– I don't always– I'm having a really shitty time right now in case you hadn't–

HARRIET: See? You see? This is– This is it exactly.

JENNA: What?

HARRIET: You're *always* having a shitty time. You're this fragile little spiky tissue paper thing we're s'posed to all look after and if we have to cancel holidays 'cause you've got dumped or if we have to rush off to hospital in the night 'cause you've got too happy with the alcopops and. And 'cause it's you, you don't just get sick and go to sleep you get fucking convulsions, or we have to spend every family meal not talking about boyfriends 'cause you're always about to break up with one, and trying not to notice when you dash straight upstairs straight after pudding then–

And now mum's disappearing and you're still fucking about like– Like it's your disaster. It's not about you now.

You haven't been to the hospital once.

JENNA: I'm scared of hospitals. Mum knows.

HARRIET: Maybe I'm scared of burial grounds. Well, here I fucking am.

JENNA: When did you start swearing?

HARRIET: Only swear when I'm really fucked off.

JENNA looks away. Pause.

JENNA: We going to come here and argue once we've buried her d'you think?

HARRIET: We're not burying her here. It's too bleak.

JENNA: Yeah, it is.

Beat.

Isn't even a bloody loo.

Beat.

Sorry. It's hard, you know?

HARRIET: Yeah.

JENNA: And I'm not. I'm not strong. You're strong.

HARRIET: Yeah.

JENNA sniffs.

JENNA: Have you got a–

HARRIET pulls a tissue out of her bag and hands it to her.

Thanks.

JENNA blows her nose. HARRIET puts the lid back on her Tupperware box and presses it down firmly at each corner. JENNA watches her.

D'you and Josh ever fight?

HARRIET sighs.

HARRIET: Is this leading into a Mark / discussion–

JENNA: No.

HARRIET: Because you know I think you should / dump–

JENNA: I just want to know if you guys ever–

HARRIET: Not everyone wants to be yelling all the time–

JENNA: I don't want to we just seem to–

HARRIET: So dump him just do it.

Beat.

JENNA: You never fight?

HARRIET: Sometimes. Rare occasions.

JENNA: About what?

HARRIET: Stupid things. Little things. Just when we're both stressed and.

JENNA: You start bitching at each other and it blows up–

HARRIET: Not like that, no.

Just like, I don't know – I don't know why I'm having to justify my relationship here – like when we were buying the house and we both really wanted it and we were scared we wouldn't get it, so. I'd go off at him about things he should have done and he'd get cross at me 'cause I didn't understand how busy he is and how he was trying to earn lots of money so we could afford it…

JENNA: How do they end?

HARRIET: I go all quiet, he hugs me and we both feel better and get on with it.

JENNA: D'you have sex afterwards?

HARRIET: Jen.

JENNA: Mum thinks we should talk about sex more.

HARRIET: Mum thinks we should spend time together.

Beat.

I think she switched your phone off deliberately.

JENNA: She couldn't have–

HARRIET: You never check it. She could have done it this morning. When you were in the shower or something.

JENNA: I don't–

HARRIET: I might be wrong.

JENNA: Never.

HARRIET: Piss off.

JENNA: How long after the fight d'you make up?

HARRIET: What?

JENNA: How long afterwards?

HARRIET: Half an hour?

JENNA: Same day.

HARRIET: Always.

JENNA frowns and looks across the field.

JENNA: D'you think we've given it long enough now?

HARRIET: I think we've established this isn't it.

JENNA: This is not it.

HARRIET: She wouldn't like it.

JENNA: I think trees are the thing. Did you see the lady at the office?

HARRIET: Said hello.

JENNA: Started telling me how long it takes to decompose. Unbelievable.

HARRIET: Mum'd love that.

JENNA: Then she said 'That's probably not what you want to hear right now'. I mean God!

HARRIET: Come on.

They start to leave. JENNA sees HARRIET's plastic bag on the stile.

JENNA: Don't forget your arse-bag.

HARRIET: How long does it take? To decompose.

JENNA: Six weeks or so.

HARRIET: Length of the school holidays.

JENNA: Yeah.

Fade.

SCENE 4

The living room. A sluggish Sunday afternoon, late November.

ALEC brings a small fan heater into the room and sets it down on the coffee table. He picks up the plug attached to the heater and looks at it.

He exits briefly, and returns, purposeful, a screwdriver in his hand. He goes to start unscrewing the plug casing, then stops. He catches the record player out of the corner of his eye.

He goes over to the record player and takes out a record from beneath it. He gently slides it out of its sleeve and blows it to remove any dust. He places the record on the turntable, then bends down to position the needle. Brahms' Hungarian Dances plays loudly, then quieter as ALEC turns down the volume, a little self-conscious.

He holds up the inner sleeve of the record, looking at the light through the translucent circle of plastic in the centre.

ALEC looks at the fan heater again, then sits down in his armchair and closes his eyes.

HARRIET enters, a cardboard box in her hand. ALEC starts when she comes in and sits up.

HARRIET: Your fridge is where food goes to die.

HARRIET brings the box into the room and puts it on the floor in front of the coffee table. She sits down next to the box.

You know there's things in there went off five years ago? I found a jar of mint jelly right at the back, expired December 1990.

ALEC: Probably still alright…

HARRIET: There's a whole new eco system starting in there.

ALEC: So not dying.

HARRIET: What?

ALEC stands up to turn off the record.

ALEC: You said food goes there to die. Starting a new eco system isn't dying.

HARRIET: Regenerating, then. You don't have to *[turn the music off]*

He lifts the needle off the record anyway.

Well I've chucked it all so at least no-one's dying of botulism.

Beat.

ALEC: What's in the box?

HARRIET: Spices cupboard. It's like an archaeological dig.

ALEC: Does your mother know / about this?

HARRIET: No. Stealth cleaning.

ALEC: She still asleep?

HARRIET: Off and on. Least she's resting. I should head home once she's up.

ALEC sits in his chair with the fan heater on the floor and the plug on his lap.

I used to worry about botulism every time we had spaghetti on toast, you know.

ALEC: Did you?

HARRIET: Dented tins. I really don't mind you having music on...

ALEC: Thought you were in the kitchen.

HARRIET: Felt like some company.

ALEC grimaces.

ALEC: You were cold.

HARRIET: It's freezing in there, dad.

ALEC: I know.

HARRIET: The freezer's got more ice on the outside than– You should get a heater in there.

ALEC points at the heater on the table.

Oh, OK.

ALEC: Can't get the bloody thing to work. Think it's the fuse. In the plug.

HARRIET: Chuck it out, get a new one. They don't cost much.

ALEC: Might as well try fixing it...

HARRIET: You're so post-war, Dad.

ALEC: Which one?

HARRIET: Crimean. When are they fixing the boiler?

ALEC: Last Thursday.

HARRIET looks at him.

They have a very, um, *fluid* relationship with time, these heating people. Our weeks of freezing to death are like five

59

minutes of sunshine on their planet. And it's a new model, which means no-one's learned how to fix it yet.

HARRIET: Why did you / buy it?

ALEC: Looked warm in the brochure.

Beat. ALEC struggles to undo one of the screws on the plug.

Dammit. God dammit.

HARRIET: You alright?

ALEC: Marvellous. (*As he unscrews.*) It's all going terribly well.

HARRIET: Where's Jen?

ALEC: Out with the boyfriend. Some kind of crisis or other.

HARRIET: She showing any sign of moving back into her flat or is she staying here forever now?

ALEC: Daren't ask.

MYRA enters, wearing a dressing gown. She hovers by the door.

MYRA: Hi.

ALEC: Sorry, did I wake you?

MYRA: Bloody pipes banging woke me. 'Marry a chartered surveyor', they said, 'least your house'll always be sound'.

Beat.

Have you seen upstairs?

HARRIET: Why?

MYRA: All the doors are open.

ALEC and HARRIET look at MYRA.

We keep the doors shut up there, don't we? We keep them shut or Baggins gets in and drops hairs all over. On the beds and everything.

We're behaving like a family without a cat. Like a non-cat family. He's only been gone a few weeks.

HARRIET: Must've been Jenna.

MYRA: It's not always Jenna.

Beat. MYRA tightens her dressing gown around her.

HARRIET: How you feeling?

MYRA: Achy.

HARRIET: Can I get you / anything?

MYRA: No. Thanks. I'm OK.

ALEC: You warm enough?

MYRA: I'm fine. God's sake.

MYRA goes into the kitchen. HARRIET watches her. ALEC goes back to unscrewing the plug.

ALEC: Always cross when she wakes up.

HARRIET: Did you do the doors?

ALEC: Can't remember.

HARRIET: I haven't been upstairs. Apart from seeing mum.

MYRA returns.

MYRA: You've thrown away all the food.

HARRIET: Only the stuff that's gone out of date.

MYRA: It was fine, you don't have to religiously–

HARRIET: Mum, there was mint jelly from 1990.

MYRA: That was fine.

HARRIET: I'd have been fifteen. In 1990. Probably me picked it up in the supermarket. Probably picked up mint jelly instead of mint sauce and that's why it stayed there all this / time.

MYRA: Exactly. There were memories in there.

HARRIET: There was bacteria in there.

MYRA: Beautiful. Circle of Life.

MYRA sighs and sits on the sofa. She tucks her legs up under her, painfully.

Ow ow ow ow ow.

The others look at her.

Fine.

ALEC: Permission to give you a blanket?

MYRA: Bugger off.

MYRA points to the box in front of HARRIET.

What's this?

HARRIET: Spice cupboard.

MYRA: Why?

HARRIET: You were asleep. Wanted to do something helpful.

MYRA: You could help me choose a reading for the funeral.

HARRIET: We can go through these together. If you like.

ALEC fumbles and drops part of the plug casing.

ALEC: Dammit.

MYRA: What are you doing?

ALEC leans down the side of his seat to pick up the part he's dropped.

ALEC: Fixing the heater, for the kitchen.

MYRA: Oh good, that's going to work.

ALEC: What's the matter with you?

MYRA: Cancer. Next question?

ALEC gets up and picks up the heater.

ALEC: I did know that. Do this somewhere else.

ALEC goes out to the kitchen.

MYRA: Careful, it's cold in there.

MYRA turns back to HARRIET.

Go on, then.

HARRIET: OK.

HARRIET takes out a jar of spice.

OK. Turmeric. April 2002.

MYRA: Keep that.

HARRIET: Three years.

MYRA: I'll hardly have opened it, there's no air in there.

HARRIET: Right. Tell you what – we'll do a keeping pile and a throwing pile, and if the keeping pile looks too big at the end we'll thin it out, alright?

MYRA: Fine.

HARRIET puts the turmeric to one side.

HARRIET: So this is the keeping pile. And rules: we chuck anything over three years old, OK?

MYRA: Great.

HARRIET takes out another jar.

HARRIET: Cayenne pepper. August 1998.

MYRA: There was something I used to make with that, what was it?

HARRIET: We're chucking it. Throwing-out pile.

HARRIET puts the cayenne at a distance from the turmeric. Picks out another jar.

Herbes De Provence.

MYRA: Oh, we should go to Provence again.

HARRIET: 1993.

HARRIET puts the jar with the cayenne on the throwing out pile. MYRA looks at the pile, wistful. HARRIET picks out another jar.

Basil. My god, 2003.

MYRA: Oh goody I can keep it.

HARRIET puts the basil on the keeping pile and goes to pick out another jar.

HARRIET: Dad was being nice. Cumin. 1989.

MYRA holds out her hand for the jar.

MYRA: Let me see.

HARRIET hands it to her.

Never used these.

MYRA hands the jar back.

I know he was being nice.

HARRIET: Chuck?

MYRA: Yes.

HARRIET takes out another.

HARRIET: 1991.

She puts it straight on the throwing-away pile. She will look at several and consign them immediately to the throwing-away pile before she next consults MYRA.

Ask him back in?

MYRA: Harriet, you can't / keep–

HARRIET: I just think–

MYRA: I'm grumpy and tired. And sick. Let me be grumpy today.

HARRIET turns back to the box.

Jenna lets me be grumpy.

HARRIET: Jenna wouldn't notice if you lost a limb.

Beat. HARRIET takes out another jar.

Paprika. '95.

MYRA: Mum used to use that. Used to sprinkle it on top of macaroni cheese. She always said paprika was great 'cause it was colourful but didn't really taste of anything. Course the answer was it didn't taste of anything in our house 'cause she'd had the jar so long.

HARRIET: You never told me that.

MYRA: Just dust now, isn't it. Chuck it. Chuck all of them, I'm not doing any more cooking.

HARRIET: Don't say that.

MYRA: It's true.

HARRIET: We'll do this another time.

HARRIET starts to hurriedly put all the jars back in the box. Even the throwing-out pile.

MYRA: You could just put a sticker or something on all the bad ones and get rid of them when I'm–

HARRIET: We'll do it another time, I've got to get home.

HARRIET finishes putting the jars in the box.

Do it later.

HARRIET picks up the box, and without looking at MYRA, exits to the kitchen.

MYRA sighs and stands up.

MYRA: Ow ow ow ow ow.

She looks around her, not sure what to do. She sees that ALEC's record is still spinning on the turntable and goes over to look at it. She looks at the label in the centre, recognises it and exhales. She stops the record spinning and closes the lid of the player.

ALEC comes to the doorway with the heater in his arms. He is hesitant.

ALEC: I can't find anywhere I'm not snapped at...

MYRA smiles at him gently.

Is it safe to come out again?

MYRA: Yes, it's safe.

ALEC comes into the room.

ALEC: Got it mended, I think.

MYRA: Well done.

ALEC sets the heater down on the table.

ALEC: Just plug it in...

ALEC goes over to the socket and inserts the plug. He looks at MYRA.

Cross your fingers.

MYRA holds up her fingers, already crossed, to show him. He moves closer to her and the heater.

MYRA: Am I horrible?

ALEC: You're ill.

MYRA squeezes ALEC's arm, just above the elbow.

Here goes.

ALEC reaches out to switch the heater on. They wait for a moment. Nothing happens.

Little light's supposed to… Check the plug's in properly.

He goes over to the plug and pushes it harder into the socket. He turns back to MYRA who puts her hand out to feel if anything's coming out of the heater.

Hot or cold?

MYRA: Nothing.

She's not sure for a second.

Hang on…

No, nothing.

Fade.

SCENE 5

A civil cemetery in Coventry, a dry but cold day in early December.

The cemetery has cordoned off a small corner of its land as a vague gesture to the natural burial movement. No-one has yet been buried here and it's not difficult to see why – the cemetery is run-down and grim, surrounded by industrial buildings. The natural burial site is little more than a patch of earth.

ALEC sits on a park bench, the Independent crossword on his lap. JENNA stands facing him, a tissue in her hand.

ALEC: Didn't you get the message?

JENNA: What message?

ALEC: Sorry, I left a message on your mobile phone.

JENNA rummages in her handbag and pulls out her mobile.

JENNA: God. Sorry. Don't always hear it in here.

She sees a message on the phone.

Um.

What did it say?

ALEC: That it'd be me and not your mother.

ALEC rubs his eyes under his glasses.

She's not brilliant today.

JENNA twists the tissue in her hands.

JENNA: Worse than this morning?

ALEC: Went back to bed about ten.

Shouldn't stay out too long.

JENNA sits down at the other end of the bench from ALEC.

JENNA: Hello Dad.

ALEC: Hello.

ALEC stands up to take off his coat. He folds it and carefully places it beside him on the bench.

JENNA: You hot?

ALEC: No, just a bit–

JENNA: Could they do better for her in the hospital? Maybe if we bullied her together...

ALEC: I don't know, love. It's up to her, isn't it?

JENNA looks around her.

JENNA: This is horrible. This is the worst–

ALEC: Why are we looking at it?

JENNA: It's the closest. On the map – my flat, your house, Harri's house. Nearest there is to equidistant.

Mum thinks we'll visit more if we're close by.

ALEC: Shall we go, then?

JENNA: Can we just– I promised we'd give each place a chance, give it a few minutes at least, not dismiss anything. Out of hand. She said you can't always tell just by looking.

ALEC: Well it's warmer than the house. Everywhere's warmer than the house.

ALEC goes back to his crossword. JENNA looks around at the burial ground.

JENNA: Is it funereal or funereal? *[fun-er-real or funereal]*

ALEC: (*Without looking up.*) Funereal. *[Funereal]*

JENNA: Always say that wrong. Like ethereal. *[eth-er-real]*

ALEC: Ethereal. *[Ethereal]*

JENNA: Yeah.

Beat.

We'll go in a minute.

ALEC: Alright.

Pause. ALEC looks up from his paper, has a vague idea he should say something.

JENNA: I saw five separate people fall over in the street today.

ALEC: Did you?

JENNA: Three of them just walking down the street, not massive arse over whatsit falling, just like when your ankle turns and you feel really stupid and you have to do a face… Then another two on the bus. I was on the bus, they were on the pavement. Started to wonder if it was me making them fall just by looking at them, like the tree falling down in a wood thing, but I tried it on lots of other people and they didn't fall over and then I got here.

Do you miss her?

ALEC: Miss her?

JENNA: Like when people say 'missing you already'. I miss her already sometimes.

It–

ALEC frowns.

Have you got anything to eat?

ALEC: No.

JENNA: Haven't had any lunch.

ALEC: Oh, hang on.

ALEC feels in his pocket and pulls out a Fry's Peppermint Cream chocolate bar. He hands it to JENNA.

JENNA: Ooh, your favourite!

ALEC: Don't tell your mother.

JENNA: I hide chocolate too.

JENNA opens the packet. She takes a piece and eats it.

Had these when you were little, didn't you? What was the other one?

ALEC: Five boys. Fry's Five Boys chocolate.

JENNA: What was that like?

ALEC: Chocolate with a picture of five boys on the top.

JENNA eats another piece of chocolate.

JENNA: D'you want some?

ALEC: No thanks love, you have it.

JENNA: Got some more in the car?

ALEC: No.

ALEC goes back to his crossword. JENNA finishes the bar of chocolate in silence.

JENNA: Can I put your coat on?

ALEC: If you want.

JENNA stands up and puts the coat on over the top of her jacket. She sits down, her arms hugging the coat around her.

JENNA: It's really cold here.

ALEC: We can go.

JENNA: In a minute.

ALEC looks up. Tries to make conversation.

ALEC: Where's Martin today?

JENNA: Mark.

ALEC: Mark.

JENNA: Think he wants to split up.

Beat. ALEC looks away, tired.

ALEC: Does he?

JENNA: Think you were right not liking him.

Pause. ALEC rubs his eyes.

ALEC: I'm sorry, I–

JENNA: No, dads aren't supposed to like the boyfriend, are they?

Just isn't nice to me anymore. Since he started this stupid course. Just– just wants to be with his stupid college friends. Some of them are like, barely twenty and he's over thirty– it's pathetic. Tells me he doesn't have enough money when I suggest we go out to eat, or go out or whatever, but he's got enough money to go to the pub after every class and–

ALEC: Maybe you just… you've just… Hmm.

JENNA frowns. ALEC looks at the sky.

JENNA: Like last week I finally persuaded him to let me meet his stupid new friends, this is after weeks of saying 'why don't I come and meet you after college' and him saying 'no, you're alright' and changing the subject and me thinking 'oh for fuck's sake!'. Sorry.

ALEC: It's all / right.

JENNA: So, I go to meet him after a seminar and talk to his friends and I thought I'd been OK, just myself, thought I made quite a good impression, you know? And then we got back to his, and he said I'd *embarrassed* him and I'd *monopolised* the conversation…

ALEC: You can get a bit…

JENNA: I feel like we're already splitting up, like I can feel it beginning to end. Sometimes I can hear the end of it in his voice.

And I get so worried about mum and stuff, you know? I need someone *there*. And then he says I'm clingy, I'm too needy. And I'm like 'what d'you expect, my mum's got cancer…'

Pause. ALEC searches for something to say.

ALEC: He's probably just… Hmm.

JENNA: We don't even have sex anymore…

ALEC: You don't have to / tell me about that.

JENNA: Sorry.

Beat.

ALEC: I can't really do…problems.

JENNA: No, sorry.

Beat. She puts her head on his shoulder. He flinches, almost imperceptibly.

ALEC: I've got to get back.

ALEC stands up.

D'you want a lift?

JENNA looks at him, then down at the ground.

JENNA: Yes please.

ALEC: I'll bring the car round.

ALEC walks off to the car park. JENNA is left watching him go. She pulls the coat around her, tightly, and looks at the cemetery, twisting her tissue.

Fade.

73

SCENE 6

The living room, Friday evening, late January.

JENNA and HARRIET sit on the sofa, their hands on their laps, silent, preoccupied, their faces disordered. Both have the slightly inflated look of wearing several layers of clothing and each has more than one scarf around her neck.

They are both staring at a white cardboard coffin, on the carpet in front of them.

Long pause.

JENNA: So that's it, then.

HARRIET: Yes.

   Pause.

JENNA: That's it.

HARRIET: Yes.

   Pause.

JENNA: That's what it looks like.

HARRIET: Yes.

   Pause.

JENNA: Looks big.

HARRIET: Sometimes fat people die.

   JENNA laughs, then stops herself.

JENNA: Wasn't very hard, was it?

HARRIET: Like IKEA.

JENNA: Funny they haven't changed the shape. Hundreds of years and they still look like that. Still looks like a coffin.

   JENNA stands up and goes to the coffin. She takes the lid off.

Need some cushions, make it nice in there.

She touches the plastic lining of the coffin. It crackles.

Know what this is?

HARRIET: What?

JENNA: Cremfilm.

HARRIET: Nice.

JENNA: Fluids.

HARRIET: Yeah.

She crackles it again.

JENNA: Think we'll get something else. Feels a bit freezer bag.

JENNA runs her fingers along the side of the coffin.

HARRIET: Does it feel strong?

JENNA: Yeah.

We should start painting.

HARRIET: Should draw it on first. With pencil.

JENNA: Shall I fetch her, show it to her?

HARRIET: D'you want to?

They consider it.

Show her later. Once we've done some drawing.

JENNA: OK.

HARRIET: Sky and stars.

JENNA: I'm shit at art.

HARRIET: Me too.

JENNA: You're not shit at anything.

75

HARRIET: I'll get pencils.

HARRIET goes to the kitchen. JENNA looks at the coffin, biting her thumbnail.

ALEC enters, holding a telephone and a piece of paper. He stops and looks at the coffin.

JENNA holds her hands out towards it, presenting it, an awkward magician.

JENNA: Ta-dah!

Pause.

ALEC: That's it then.

JENNA: Yeah.

Pause.

ALEC: Good. Good Lord.

ALEC looks around the room, anywhere but the coffin.

I'm looking for my– Ah.

He sees his pullover on his armchair.

There we are.

He picks up the pullover to wear over the top of the one he's wearing already. He pulls it on sleeves first, then head.

He looks at the phone.

Right.

He starts to tap in a number, from the piece of paper in his hand.

JENNA: Who you ringing?

ALEC: Boiler people. Give them a piece of my mind.

JENNA: Good luck.

ALEC finishes tapping in the number and listens to it ringing.

HARRIET returns with two pencils.

HARRIET: Sorry, lots of crap in the pencil drawer.

She hands one to JENNA and looks enquiringly at ALEC.

ALEC: On hold.

JENNA: Boiler firm.

ALEC: Vivaldi. Spring.

HARRIET: Brilliant.

ALEC tries to stay turned away from the coffin but keeps catching it out of the corner of his eye. JENNA watches him.

So what we doing?

JENNA: (*Points to the feet end of the coffin.*) Sky. (*And to the head end.*) Stars.

HARRIET: That way round?

JENNA: Don't want stars round her feet, do we?

HARRIET: So she's what, standing on a cloud? Just get her a harp and be done with it.

JENNA: What she asked for.

HARRIET: So clouds down here, stars up here...

ALEC: Is that what she wants on it, clouds and stars?

JENNA: Something like that.

ALEC stares at the coffin. He starts as someone answers the phone.

ALEC: Oh, um, sorry– Sorry, can I–

Can I call you back?

He hangs up, quickly. Sees the others watching him.

Do it later. Have to be in the right mood.

HARRIET and JENNA turn back to the coffin. ALEC edges towards it.

So how much did it– How much did it cost, this?

JENNA: 'Bout seventy pounds.

ALEC: Well. Bargain.

HARRIET: I'll start on the sky, yeah? Think I can do clouds.

JENNA: I'll do stars.

HARRIET and JENNA tentatively start to draw on the coffin.

ALEC: Is that what they– Do they all cost that?

JENNA: Approximately. Not a very competitive market.

ALEC: Does a more. Expensive one look. Look less like a cardboard box?

JENNA: Won't look like a box when it's painted.

ALEC: Doesn't look strong enough.

JENNA: We're not the first people to ever use one.

ALEC: No.

JENNA: We could test it.

ALEC: No, I don't think so.

ALEC paces around the coffin.

What's that inside it?

JENNA: Cremfilm.

ALEC: For the, um–

JENNA: Fluids.

ALEC: Right.

ALEC looks out of the window.

Right.

HARRIET and JENNA look at each other. An awkward pause.

HARRIET: I've got a new game, Dad.

ALEC: Have you, love?

HARRIET: Josh thought of it. We were talking about cocoa farmers.

JENNA sniggers.

Shut up. About what a shitty time they have and stuff, and then Josh says he's never seen a cocoa bean. Which is stupid because he's been everywhere. Like he doesn't know what one looks like, he just knows the word, knows what they are. So we started a game of thinking of things you've never seen.

ALEC: Hmm.

HARRIET: D'you know what I mean? Not like an elephant because you might not actually have *seen* an elephant but you know what it looks like 'cause you've seen pictures – something you have no idea what it looks like but you know the word for.

ALEC: A competent boiler engineer. D'you see the one they sent last week? Must've been about fourteen. Promise they're sending round someone decent, someone with half a whatsit, then you open the door and you can tell straight off. Different monkey, same zoo…

Good game.

Short pause.

JENNA: Don't think I've ever seen a carburettor.

ALEC: You must / have.

JENNA: No, I haven't, I'm sure I haven't.

HARRIET: Isn't that the bit, the bit attached to the / exhaust pipe?

ALEC: Exhaust pipe. The wider bit.

JENNA: Is it? Oh, I've seen that, is that what it is?

ALEC: Yes.

JENNA: OK.

Pause. They think.

I've never seen a slide rule.

HARRIET: Oh, good one.

JENNA: No mental picture.

ALEC: It's like a– I've got one, actually.

JENNA: See, I didn't even know it was small enough to go in a house.

ALEC: Upstairs somewhere. I could dig it out. I'll go and–

JENNA: Dad, it's / OK.

ALEC: In the study I think.

ALEC leaves.

HARRIET: Go and have a look.

JENNA: We're doing this.

HARRIET: Make him happy, he likes showing things.

JENNA: He'll bring it down if he finds it.

They continue to draw.

Is this how it'll be, d'you think? The three of us.

HARRIET: Don't know.

Beat.

JENNA: What was your thing?

HARRIET: What?

JENNA: Thing you'd never seen.

HARRIET: Oh. Big one. Never seen a dead body.

Pause. JENNA thinks.

JENNA: Yeah, but that doesn't fit, does it? With the game. You know what that's going to look like. It'll look like mum.

HARRIET puts down her pencil.

HARRIET: These clouds look like turds.

JENNA looks.

I'd have learned to draw properly, you know, if I'd known…

They examine their work so far.

JENNA: You know what Baggins'd do? He'd get in there, curl up and have a sleep. Loved boxes.

HARRIET: 'My cat likes to hide in boxes'.

JENNA: Wouldn't even be bothered what it's for.

They look at the coffin, then at each other.

HARRIET: You.

JENNA: No, you.

HARRIET: You.

JENNA: You're the oldest.

HARRIET: You're the naughtiest.

JENNA: You won't be cross?

HARRIET: Why would I be cross?

JENNA: You know, all self-righteous like 'ooh, you shouldn't have done that'.

HARRIET: No.

JENNA: OK.

JENNA steps gingerly into the coffin. She sits down, pulling her knees up under her chin. HARRIET watches her, intently.

HARRIET: Lie down.

JENNA: Might snag the Cremfilm.

HARRIET: Go on.

JENNA looks at HARRIET, then lies down slowly.

How is it?

JENNA: Twenty years ago you'd have put the lid on and sat on it.

Beat.

Never looked at this ceiling before, looks fucking awful. Look at that crack.

JENNA's hand comes up out of the coffin, pointing.

Place is falling to bits.

HARRIET hears a noise, off. JENNA sits up and looks around.

HARRIET: Coming downstairs.

JENNA clambers hastily out of the coffin. They look at each other.

JENNA: This didn't happen. We didn't do this.

HARRIET: No, that'd be–

JENNA: Wrong. Morbid.

ALEC returns, shaking his head.

ALEC: Couldn't find it. Buried under years of crap.

HARRIET: Another time.

ALEC: Your mother's coming down, she's woken up.

HARRIET: Right. Great.

ALEC paces, rattling the change in his pockets. JENNA shivers.

ALEC: You're not going to do anything–

JENNA: What?

ALEC: Alarming.

JENNA: Not about me, is it?

MYRA comes in, rubbing sleep from her eyes, slightly dopey. The others all look at her.

MYRA: Let me see it.

The others move away so that MYRA has a clear view of the coffin. MYRA looks at it. She wakes up. Looks at it for a long time.

That's it, then.

Pause.

Was it difficult?

HARRIET: Instructions were good, very clear.

JENNA: You need them clear, don't you, I mean it's a difficult time, you don't want to be…

MYRA continues to look at the coffin without moving towards it.

It'll look better once it's painted. Once Harriet learns to draw clouds.

MYRA: Thought I was painting it.

JENNA: Well, if that's what you– I just thought–

MYRA: I'll paint it.

MYRA frowns.

Doesn't look how I thought.

JENNA: It's good and strong.

ALEC: What did you expect, a Wendy house?

MYRA: Doesn't look very wide.

JENNA: It's wider than you, we measured when we ordered it.

Pause.

MYRA: I think I'd like to be buried on my side.

HARRIET: On your side?

MYRA: Like the way I sleep. On my side. With my legs tucked up. My hands under my / face

MYRA mimes where her hands would go.

ALEC: Oh for God's / sake!

MYRA: So it's like going to sleep. What?

ALEC: Just rewrite the whole bloody–

MYRA: I just think I'd be less. Less scared of the earth.

ALEC: You won't be conscious.

MYRA: All that earth coming down. On top of me.

ALEC: It doesn't make any / difference…

MYRA: Wouldn't you be scared?

Beat. She looks at the three of them.

D'you know what I read today? Something I never knew. Never knew before.

When you die, if you've eaten, if you've got any food in in your system, in your *bowels*, horrible word– When you die, all your muscles relax. Including your, your rectum. So if there's. If there's anything *there* when you die, next thing you do is um is shit. After you die, you can shit. I might die while you're all out of the house and you might come home and find me covered in– Your last picture of me.

I won't, you're right Alec, I won't know about it. Still can't bear it.

The others watch her, paralysed. MYRA looks at her family.

Look at you.

Will one of you please for a bloody change know what to do?

Pause.

HARRIET goes to MYRA and puts her arms around her. MYRA looks at ALEC over HARRIET's shoulder.

Fade.

SCENE 7

A burial ground in Coventry. Wednesday afternoon, the kind of surprisingly warm mid-March day that provokes premature summer behaviour. This is a mature woodland which has only recently been converted into a burial site. Graves are placed between the trees, with no markers except for a small plaque on a tree close to each grave. The ground under the trees is carpeted with moss and there are daffodils and crocuses.

JENNA sits under a tree, looking around her, smoking.

HARRIET enters, a little dishevelled. JENNA looks up and sees her.

JENNA: Oh, for fuck's sake.

HARRIET: What?

85

JENNA: It's supposed to be mum. Does she have to keep sending proxies? I know what she's doing, I'm not a fucking social cripple and my phone's been on all morning 'cause I checked it, before you start.

HARRIET looks at the back of her hands.

HARRIET: Said she's fed up of us coming home saying they're not right. Says she doesn't need to see them if they're all going to be not right.

JENNA: But I think this one might be.

HARRIET: Really?

JENNA: Yeah.

HARRIET looks around her.

HARRIET: Yeah. Proper wood.

JENNA: Be gorgeous in summer. The crocuses are nice.

HARRIET: Croci. *[Croaky]*

JENNA: (*In a croaky voice.*) The crocuses are nice.

HARRIET: Oh, funny.

JENNA has to cough to clear her throat.

JENNA: 'Scuse me. I bet there's bluebells. I bet it's all covered in bluebells in the summer.

Beat.

HARRIET: I don't want it to be summer.

JENNA: How d'you mean?

HARRIET: When she dies. Winter's easier, everyone's all bundled up, rushing around busy and no one has to ask you, you don't get *asked*...

Summer you're supposed to be happy, aren't you? People being happy all over the place, it's all warm, you – can't wear your scarf anymore. Couples all over the place, all being new with each other, all happy and *new*...

JENNA: You alright?

HARRIET looks at JENNA, then away.

HARRIET: No. No, I'm losing it. Quite successfully.

HARRIET looks at JENNA, smiles weakly.

Doesn't matter. It's not about me.

JENNA: How losing it?

HARRIET scratches the backs of her hands as she speaks.

HARRIET: Just– Not being able to– Feels like– I don't know, you know how sometimes you're doing laundry and you'll– You take it all out the machine and for some reason you've left the basket somewhere else so you have to carry it all up the stairs in your arms and–

JENNA: I haven't got stairs.

HARRIET: What?

JENNA: Moved out of mum's yesterday.

HARRIET: Oh. Really? Wow. Really?

JENNA: Back in my flat now.

HARRIET: OK.

JENNA: Laundry.

HARRIET: Yeah. So I'm trying to carry it all up the stairs. And. And it's quite a big pile and I can't see where my feet are on the steps 'cause it's so big so I'm slow... But then one sock falls off the top of the pile and I bend down to pick it up but while I'm doing that something else falls and I can't pick each thing up without dropping something else and then. Before I know it I've tripped up a step and there's washing all over the floor.

Except it's not washing, it's me all over the floor.

But hey ho.

HARRIET smiles sadly and shakes her head.

And I've got this stupid eczema or something– never had eczema– backs of my hands keep itching all the time…

Are the graves under the trees?

JENNA: Spaces between. Trees are too old, aren't they?

HARRIET: Oh yeah.

JENNA: Little marker on each one to say who's there, look. (*She twists round to look at the tree behind her.*) …Dorothy Hutchins. Must have been old, don't get kids called Dorothy, do you? Hope there's no babies…

E45 cream. Stop it itching.

HARRIET paces, animated, slightly off-balance.

HARRIET: You know, I went to mum's the other day, just to check up on her and stuff. Walked in and she's sat in the coffin. Middle of the living room floor and she's– She's watching 'Have I Got News For You' and she's laughing. Sitting in it, laughing. And I just thought God, I can't cope with this I can't do this. I was looking at her and I missed her.

Don't know what I'm going to do. It hurts behind my eyes. Got this stupid eczema. My mouth keeps tasting of blood and it's not bleeding gums 'cause I thought it must be and I went to the dentist.

HARRIET stares into the distance, her hand to her mouth.

JENNA: I've got Tic-Tacs.

HARRIET: Yeah?

JENNA: Want one?

HARRIET: Please.

JENNA pulls a box of Tic-Tacs out of her bag and holds them out. HARRIET goes to her and takes the box.

JENNA: Have two if you like. Should carry Tic-Tacs. Or gum. Minty stuff's good, it makes you concentrate on it, you stop thinking about whatever you're thinking about and start thinking of. Mint.

HARRIET takes two and hands the box back.

HARRIET: Thanks.

JENNA: Better?

HARRIET paces again.

HARRIET: Yeah. I keep– I can't– Can't stop *feeling*. Can't get on with my life because I'm *feeling* all the time. Can't do anything. Keep crying. Or thinking I'm going to cry and then not being able to do anything in case I do.

Josh thinks I need to (*imitating his voice.*) 'go and talk to someone'. Which just makes me think 'What the fuck are you there for, then?'.

JENNA: Are you going to? Talk to someone.

HARRIET: Don't know. Usually I'd talk to / mum.

JENNA: Mum. Yeah.

Beat.

HARRIET: Think I'll sit down now.

JENNA: You'll get a wet arse.

HARRIET sits next to JENNA.

89

You could talk to me. If you want to. I mean, I won't be
upset if you– Know I'm less use than a snot rag in most.
Situations. But. You know…

HARRIET: Yeah.

JENNA: Everyone thinks I'm mad as a bucket, complete
liability but– Not always.

HARRIET: Thanks.

Beat.

JENNA: I finished with Mark.

HARRIET: You?

JENNA: Yup.

HARRIET: Why?

JENNA: Just– It's really boring. Just I realised I didn't want him
at the funeral. Then I thought about it some more and I
realised I didn't want *him*.

HARRIET: God. How are you?

JENNA: Oh, you know. Miss him.

HARRIET: When was this?

JENNA: Last week. Week ago.

HARRIET: What's mum think?

JENNA: Haven't told her. Didn't tell anyone.

HARRIET looks at her.

Thought I should have a practice.

JENNA takes out her Tic-Tacs and eats one.

Pause.

HARRIET stands up.

HARRIET: I've got a wet arse.

JENNA: That's awful, isn't it? Practising.

HARRIET: No, it–

   Pause.

   JENNA looks at the floor.

JENNA: The moss is nice. I like the moss.

HARRIET: Yeah. Furry.

JENNA: Warm. Like a blanket.

   Beat.

HARRIET: I need to go.

JENNA: OK.

   Beat. HARRIET looks around.

HARRIET: Yeah.

JENNA: OK.

   JENNA stands up for the first time, revealing the plastic bag she's been sitting on. She folds it up carefully and puts it into her handbag. HARRIET watches her, surprised. JENNA looks up and sees HARRIET watching.

   What?

   HARRIET laughs.

   What?

   Fade.

SCENE 8

The living room, early evening, mid-March. MYRA's cardboard coffin, now half-painted with sky and stars, is at the side of the sofa, its lid lying beside it.

ALEC has the phone in his hand and is pacing up and down. He holds a letter, which he refers to occasionally.

ALEC: The reference number at the *bottom* of the page?
...LS23161701... Mr A. Bradley, 26 Morris Avenue, look you know who I am we've been on the phone all bloody week...

Right. I've got a letter in my hand saying you were going to come round today and sort it out... Oh yes, someone came, someone came and scratched his head at it, had a cup of tea, said he couldn't fix it and toddled off again. Which to be honest isn't what I had in mind.

Listen, mate– I'm sorry, do you mind if I call you mate, it's not a word I'd normally use, but I feel we've spent a lot of time together now... Richard. Right. Richard. Richard, when are you going to fix my boiler?... Alright, try again: when– *specifically,* in *time* – are you going to fix my boiler?

... Mmm, uh huh... Do you know I have never encountered incompetence on this level before? My daughter has this thing she says (she's twenty-seven she talks like a teenager) the thing she keeps saying is 'next-level', everything's next-level wrong, next-level horrid, next-level stupid. Well this is next-level farcical if that's not a tautology.

...*Tautology.* It means– It doesn't matter... Could you just– Could you *let* me complain at you, I'm afraid I won't feel complete until I've ruined your day too. I mean what is the *point*, what is the blasted point of making a boiler so high-tech there's only two chaps in the country can fix it? What is the bloody point?... So if you agree why can't you do something about it? Somebody somewhere in your company has to take responsibility–

How many people where you're working, Richard? …How many can you see? …Where are you?… Good God, no wonder you don't care about my problems if you're in *Glasgow*.

Right, so I'm imagining, if the world's a fair place, that the others are spending a good portion of their time being screamed at by someone like me I mean I can't believe I'm completely alone in this… So what if you get everyone together and count up the amount of time you've spent listening to complaints about the CH 2010, which incidentally isn't the year you're going to fix my boiler in, and then you might work out there's a health and safety issue, something about stress and eardrums and you can all take your headpieces off and go over and tell the supervisor and maybe if you all club together and do something about it you might have the–

Hmm.

ALEC stops. He takes his glasses off and rubs his eyes.

No, that's crap. Don't have the power to do anything, do you?

ALEC paces around the coffin, looking at it.

We've been cold for four months. You know how cold a house gets after that long? Nothing residual left.

Tell you something else – my wife is dying… No– no, it's not your fault. …Cancer. Bone cancer… No, she's going to die.

So you can imagine how this is making me weary. I am spending precious hours of her dwindling life talking to you. She wants to stay at home, she doesn't want to die in hospital, she wants to die at home, which between you and me I think is a drastically bad idea, but that's what she wants and by Christ I'll get it for her if I have to come to Glasgow and do the bloody training course myself.

…No, I'm a. I'm a chartered surveyor… No, we don't do heating systems.

…Look, what it boils down to, excuse the pun, in essence what I'm saying here is the least you can do is let her die in the *warm*. It's bafflingly little to ask.

ALEC stands in the coffin.

…When? …DID YOU NOT HEAR A WORD I SAID? I want someone out here tomorrow, Richard. Tomorrow morning.

MYRA enters carrying a pot of silver paint, which she stirs with a small paintbrush. She is wearing her dressing gown.

…Yes, Thursday should be fine. Yes, two o'clock.

ALEC hangs up the phone. He takes a breath.

Thursday.

MYRA: I heard.

ALEC: House is falling apart.

MYRA: You could move.

ALEC steps out of the coffin and moves away.

ALEC: The walls are bowing.

MYRA laughs.

MYRA: It's aching. Heaving, like when you cry. Like when a person who cries, cries.

ALEC: Just years of neglect, love.

ALEC rubs his eyes under his glasses. He sits down in his chair.

Nice bath?

MYRA eases herself down by the coffin. ALEC watches the pain in her movements.

MYRA: Alright. Didn't stay in long, too much Radox, got a bit gritty.

Going off baths, too much thinking time.

She starts to add another coat of paint to the silver stars on the coffin.

ALEC: You think I should move house?

MYRA: Up to you.

She paints. Pause.

Alec, when I'm gone–

ALEC: I don't want to talk about– / I shouldn't have–

MYRA: Something really important I–

ALEC: Sleep on your side, fine, I don't care, do whatever–

MYRA: Not that something else.

ALEC looks at her, confused.

I have to– Something I have to–

You might meet someone else.

ALEC: What?

MYRA: Once I've gone. You might meet someone, you might want to–

ALEC goes to speak.

(*Stopping him.*) No please don't please don't. (*Continuing.*) You might find you– There might be some part of you that, that *can't*, because you feel I wouldn't– That it'd be… You might hold back from it, you might not even– and I– I want you to *know* that's not what I want for you.

Beat.

ALEC: Christ, Myra.

MYRA: You just don't know, do you? I mean, she might just turn up one day, just like that, out of the blue. And if she does, when she does, I don't want you to feel you can't– can't say hello.

ALEC shifts in his chair.

You're not expecting it now, but–

Alec, you could fall in love! You could fall so much in love, you could feel something *violent.* And you've got to be brave and and um *go for it* because that's what I want you to do.

In that situation. Or even. Even if it's not violent I mean. There's no reason to be alone you're too young to–

ALEC stands up. He goes over to the window and takes his handkerchief out of his pocket. He wipes his eyes, facing away from MYRA. A long pause.

ALEC: When did– When did we– When did we stop fighting this and just accept it?

MYRA goes back to painting.

MYRA: You know, you should switch to paper hankies. Women don't like those.

Beat.

ALEC: When did we decide you weren't ever–

MYRA continues painting.

I can't remember that talk, I don't remember us deciding…

MYRA: You could just say thank you.

Beat.

Thank you for arranging everything. Thank you for making sure everything's covered, not– Not forgetting anything, forgetting to say anything.

Long pause. ALEC looks out of the window, composes himself, softens.

ALEC: Thank you.

He tries to find words.

You know the funeral isn't. Isn't for you. It's for us.

Maybe if you could leave us, maybe something to do. To be– To be occupied with. After you– People need something to do.

MYRA sits still. She puts the paintbrush down.

Something to do.

ALEC goes to his chair and picks up a book from beside it. He is about to sit down, then changes his mind and goes to sit down on one end of the sofa, closer to where MYRA is. He opens his book and starts to read.

MYRA: I'm sorry.

ALEC looks over the top of his glasses at MYRA.

Thank you for sorting out the boiler. That was–

ALEC: Least I could do.

ALEC looks back at his book. A sad smile breaks MYRA's face. She comes closer to ALEC and sits next to him. Hesitant, she takes his arm and puts it around her shoulder, leaning her back against his side and pulling her feet up so that she is sitting lengthways on the sofa. She almost daren't breathe in case he notices and shrugs her away. ALEC tenses, then relaxes. He continues to read, trying to turn the pages with one hand.

MYRA: Look after the girls, won't you?

ALEC looks up.

ALEC: Are you–

MYRA: What?

ALEC: All this talk, are you thinking it's tonight or–

MYRA: Oh no. No, weeks left. Lots more awkward talks.

Pause. ALEC goes back to his book.

When my dad died, mum said she'd woken up sometimes afterwards and felt him in the room. Felt him sit down. On the edge of the bed, an actual weight. A presence. She was awake, she wasn't even–

But then I haven't sat on your bed for years, so…

ALEC gives up and closes the book, placing it on the arm of the sofa beside him. He takes off his glasses and places them on top of the book.

Maybe tonight?

She leans her head back on his shoulder. ALEC plants a gentle kiss on top of MYRA's head.

Pause.

ALEC: You know I– I do um. Cry. I will, when you–

You mustn't think I I won't.

Pause.

MYRA: OK.

Pause.

ALEC: Help you upstairs…

MYRA: No, stay here a minute. Liking this.

ALEC puts his other arm around her and holds her tight.

ALEC: My room or your room?

MYRA laughs.

MYRA: Yours is tidier.

Fade.

SCENE 9

The same burial ground as in scene 7, but now, in late March, the crocuses and daffodils are in full bloom and the morning sunlight is partially obscured by new leaves on the trees. The site has increased in beauty since we last saw it.

MYRA and JENNA stand surveying the site. MYRA is wearing a coat, JENNA isn't. JENNA carries a blanket under her arm.

JENNA: Here?

MYRA: Here.

JENNA: I think so. I think it's–

MYRA: Yes. Yes it is.

Pause. JENNA looks off.

JENNA: Is Harri coming?

MYRA: Said she wanted to stay in the car.

JENNA: OK.

JENNA takes the blanket and spreads it out on the ground.

Get you sat down.

MYRA: Can I sit on the moss?

JENNA: Um, I gue– (*She touches the moss with the palm of her hand.*) Yes, it's dry.

JENNA helps MYRA to sit down on the floor. JENNA stands up again and looks at MYRA, curious.

MYRA: What?

JENNA: You didn't make a noise. When you sat down.

MYRA: Full to my earlobes with painkillers, love.

JENNA: Right.

MYRA: I'm not getting / better–

JENNA: No, I know.

Pause.

MYRA: Should have died last Thursday. If it was six months.

JENNA: But you didn't.

MYRA: Bit busy that day. Postponed it.

MYRA laughs.

I haven't been counting or anything. Not really, I just. I looked at the dates when they first told me. It's not like they say 'you've got until the twenty second of March' or something, I just looked at the dates, so–

Yes. Think we'll know about it before it happens – all that standing round my bed bit to get through yet… Need to buy a big nightie.

JENNA: I'll get you a big nightie. M&S.

MYRA: Thanks. Anyhow, all of this is extra. All of this is better than expected.

JENNA: Yeah.

MYRA: Except I've been having headaches.

JENNA: Right. Which means–

MYRA: Skull.

They think.

JENNA: Should've brought some sandwiches.

MYRA: I'm sorry, I didn't / think–

JENNA: No, I mean, I should have. Not your job anymore. I mean, I don't mean– I mean I should've thought of it.

MYRA: Should've brought champagne. Celebrate finding this place, it's gorgeous.

JENNA: Yeah.

MYRA: I could be really happy here. Could really be beautiful.

Beat. JENNA thinks.

JENNA: What food d'you want? At the funeral, you know, we haven't talked about– What?

MYRA is laughing.

MYRA: I hadn't– I hadn't even thought about– (*Stops herself laughing.*) You choose. I won't have to eat it. Choose something you like.

JENNA: OK. I mean, I might not eat anything, I might not feel like it…

MYRA: I brought something for you…

MYRA looks in her handbag and pulls out a business card. She hands it to JENNA.

JENNA: Who's this?

MYRA: She was at the hospital. Does green funerals. No, I know we're all sorted out but if there's anything we've forgotten. Or you want to talk to someone or–

I wouldn't mind if you called her.

JENNA: Mum, we can manage it…

MYRA: But you might feel. I don't know. Alone with it. Like the old bitch has died and now you've got to deal with all this paperwork or whatever… You might need someone.

JENNA: I know we've made it look really difficult, but–

MYRA: It's not a criticism.

JENNA turns away, putting the business card in the back pocket of her trousers.

JENNA: I thought of something we could throw in.

MYRA: Oh yes?

JENNA: Instead of flowers or your stupid glitter idea.

MYRA: What?

JENNA: Leaf skeletons. That could be beautiful.

MYRA: Yes.

JENNA: Might kind of. Float.

JENNA paces. She smiles.

MYRA: What is it?

JENNA: Nothing. You warm enough?

MYRA: Toasty. Lovely day. Glad I didn't die in winter. Less chance of the funeral getting rained on now. Couldn't bear it if you all had to carry umbrellas, want you to see each others' faces. Easier to be *open* in summer, isn't it?

Pause.

JENNA: I don't know how open we're going to be, mum. It doesn't feel– Easy. To learn. I think you want the three of us to have this fully-functioning– Talking thing. And I don't know if we will. 'Cause we never have.

I used to notice, going to the loo in the middle of the night, I'd be walking down a corridor of closed doors. Like a hotel. Four separate people.

That time I moved back in, before Christmas, I tried leaving all the doors open, see if it'd help. I'd go upstairs and open all the doors. And someone else would always go round and close them all again.

So I don't know if– If we never had that even with you here, I don't know if we'll do it without you.

MYRA strokes the moss on the ground beside her.

Sorry.

JENNA sits down beside MYRA. She bites her thumbnail. Then she catches sight of something on MYRA's skirt.

Look.

MYRA: What?

JENNA: Cat hair.

MYRA peers at it. JENNA carefully picks it off.

That's Baggins.

MYRA: Is it?

JENNA: Ginger at the tip and white at the bottom. Definitely him.

MYRA: Shows how long ago I washed it. Miss that cat.

Beat. They look at the cat hair.

JENNA: I'm really sorry.

MYRA: Blow it. Make a wish.

JENNA: That's eyelashes, isn't it?

MYRA: Blow it anyway.

JENNA does.

Don't tell me. Hope you get it.

MYRA brushes down her skirt, removing any other hairs.

I know it's not going to be perfect the three of you but– I know that.

God, if you turn into the Waltons the second I'm gone I'll be really cross 'cause I'll just think why couldn't you do that years ago, why couldn't we all enjoy that together?

But–

You don't know what you can do. Look at you – you left him all by yourself and you survived it and now look at you, you're smiling all over the place...

JENNA: Yeah.

MYRA: I mean I. I think you might be able to manage without me.

JENNA: Oh mum, I.

MYRA: Which is OK.

JENNA looks away.

Tell you something. When I first met your dad, he wouldn't– He wouldn't listen to music if there was anyone else there. Hated it, had to leave the room, wouldn't go to the opera or anything. Get up and turn the record off if you walked in. Hated it if you came in quietly and caught him. Used to drive me up the wall.

All this going to concerts business, it's all quite new. Only the last what, fifteen years or so. When Harriet started playing the silly cello, that's when it started. Knew I'd never sit through a whole concerto so he had to do it. But before that, only if he was on his own.

Beat.

You'd never have known that.

JENNA: No.

MYRA: So he's come on, you see. Since then. You know, there's always room for– Things are possible. People can–

Maybe we shouldn't have Brahms at the funeral. Might be too much.

JENNA: How is he? Is he OK?

MYRA: He's got the boiler fixed. Which is a relief, you know, now the weather's warmer anyway…

They laugh.

Now he can get on with worrying about the walls bowing and the roof leaking and the pipes banging and all the rest…

And he's going to be fine. Harri's going to be fine in a bit. You're all going to be fine, it's exciting and I won't bloody well be here to see it.

Beat.

Time is it?

JENNA: Twelve.

MYRA: Tablet time.

MYRA looks in her handbag.

Left them in the car.

JENNA: I'll get them. Then we don't have to leave yet.

MYRA: Could you bring the water as well?

JENNA: Sure.

MYRA: And Harri, maybe?

JENNA: Give it a go.

JENNA is about to go. She sees the blanket.

Take this thing back if we're not sitting on it.

She bends down to fold up the blanket. MYRA catches her smiling as she does it.

MYRA: Is it something specific you're smiling about?

JENNA: Not smiling.

MYRA: It's OK to smile.

JENNA stands up, the blanket clutched to her.

JENNA: OK.

New man.

MYRA looks at her, surprised.

Yeah.

MYRA: Who is he?

JENNA: He's not a wanker.

MYRA: Good lord.

JENNA: He's– God, there's too much to–

MYRA: How's the sex?

JENNA: Amazing. He's so, um– We didn't do it till the fourth night. I've got this– this pulse in my bottom lip all the time.

He's just– You need your tablets.

JENNA goes to leave.

I'll be quick. Don't go anywhere.

MYRA: Make pretty slow progress if I did.

JENNA: Stay there. Try not to die.

MYRA laughs.

I mean it, I haven't finished telling you.

JENNA leaves.

MYRA looks around her, smiling quietly. She slowly lies down on her side, and strokes the moss with her hand. She tucks her feet up and places her hands under her face, as if she were asleep.

After a few moments, MYRA changes her mind. She rolls over slowly and lies on her back, looking up at the sky.

Fade.

The End.

BREATHING CORPSES

When a man has lost all happiness, he's not alive.
Call him a breathing corpse.

SOPHOCLES

ACKNOWLEDGEMENTS

My heartfelt gratitude to these people, who were crucial to the development of *Breathing Corpses*: Charlotte Mann and Rod Hall; Tamara Harvey; Jack Thorne; Michael Shaw; Tina and Stuart Wade; Nina Steiger; Sacha Wares; Nina Lyndon, Emily McLaughlin, Simon Stephens and the Royal Court YWP; Nikolas Kamtsis and all at Interplay Europe 2004; Neil McPherson; Jack Andrews and the Pearson Playwrights panel; plus Anna Mackmin, Ian Rickson, Graham Whybrow and all at the Royal Court.

Thank you.

LW, February 2005

Characters

AMY
19, a hotel chambermaid

JIM
45, manager of a self-storage facility

ELAINE
46, Jim's wife

RAY
26, an employee at Jim's self-storage site

KATE
35, runs her own business

BEN
28, Kate's live-in boyfriend

CHARLIE
30, a hotel guest

Breathing Corpses was first performed on 24 February 2005 at the Royal Court Jerwood Theatre Upstairs with the following company:

AMY, Laura Elphinstone

JIM, Paul Copley

ELAINE, Niamh Cusack

RAY, Ryan Pope

KATE, Tamzin Outhwaite

BEN, James McAvoy

CHARLIE, Rupert Evans

Director, Anna Mackmin

Designer, Paul Wills

Lighting Designer, Mark Jonathan

Sound Designer, Ian Dickinson

SCENE 1

Tuesday morning, late January, cold but bright.

A hotel room. Not a great hotel, a mid-price hotel that trades on its views over the town rather than its quality of service.

Someone is lying in the bed, the sheets pulled up high. The figure is absolutely motionless.

AMY comes into the room with clean towels over her arm and a plastic carry-case of cleaning fluids. She is wearing a black skirt and white shirt, with a burgundy tabard over the top. She has rubber gloves on her hands.

She stops short when she sees there is someone in the bed.

AMY: Oh god, sorry.

> *She goes to back out of the room, then stops again. She turns back slowly for a longer look at the figure in the bed.*

Right.

God not again.

> *She looks away. Bites her lip.*

You're supposed to put the Do Not Disturb on. Then I wouldn't come barging in.

> *AMY takes a breath and goes over to the bed. She lifts the sheet and looks under it.*

OK.

> *She replaces the sheet. She sees a pill bottle on the bedside table and picks it up. It's empty.*

OK.

> *Beat.*

> *AMY lifts the sheet and puts one of her hands to the forehead of the body underneath. She frowns, unable to feel the temperature through her gloves.*

She takes off one glove and touches the forehead with her hand.

Yeah.

She lifts the figure's arm out from under the sheet and puts her fingers to its wrist. She looks at her watch with her other hand. A moment.

Yeah.

She lets the arm drop and it falls, lifeless. She watches, interested, then picks it up again and drops it. And again.

Yep.

AMY carefully puts the arm back under the sheet. She puts her rubber glove back on.

She goes over to the dressing table and sits on the stool, looking at the bed. She puts a hand to her mouth and looks around the room.

She goes to the phone by the side of the bed and picks it up, never taking her eyes off the body. She starts to dial, then changes her mind and puts the receiver down.

She sits back down on the stool and makes a sound like crying. She stops herself almost instantly.

Shit. Sorry. Sorry.

She looks to the bed momentarily, as if the corpse said something.

I'm OK.

AMY wipes her eyes and smiles.

Just– you're dead and I'm going to get sacked I think, so– Not very– not very good, is it?

She laughs at herself.

Talking to you.

She frowns, looking around the room.

That's new.

She turns back to the corpse.

What's your name, Mr Man?

She turns back to the bed, as if the corpse spoke.

I'll go down and tell them in a minute. Probably think I'm joking this time.

Beat.

AMY sees an envelope propped up on the dressing table.

Oh, you did a letter. Nice.

AMY picks the envelope up.

You know you look– I bet you were lovely. I bet you were really– really kind.

Not a person I'd ever really talk to but. But you look lovely. Don't fancy you or anything, you're a bit old for me. Probably got kids my age. Oh god have you got–

Beat. She looks at the envelope.

Does it say in here? Who's Elaine?

She turns the envelope over in her hand.

You didn't lick it. You know they'll take this. Evidence. She'll not get it for days. She'll have a few days of not knowing why, while they're doing tests on it and stuff. If you've said why in here.

D'you mind if I– It's just you've not sealed it, so no-one'd know, cept you and me and I won't tell anyone if you don't.

AMY opens the letter and turns it over to see the name at the bottom.

Jim. Hi Jim.

She reads the letter.

Oh my god. A woman in a *box*. Like a cardboard box? God. Yeah, that's really hard. Hard enough finding you, can't imagine if I found one in a box.

Didn't you wonder about who was going to find you?

AMY finishes the letter.

That's a really nice letter, Jim. I mean, you know... For that kind of letter it's nice. Not too long, you don't blame anyone. Wouldn't seem fair, really, they never get chance to say anything back. Good you haven't blamed anyone.

D'you mind if I open the window? It's just you smell a bit. No offence, but. It's just– You've had a stressful time, what with the– (*Gestures to the letter.*) and I think you've– on the sheets, so–

She opens the window.

Cold out there.

Don't want to smell nasty when they come in, do you? Least it's winter, you'd smell worse if it was summer. Did you mean to wait till after Christmas, did you think about that?

AMY looks out of the window.

See the park from here. Best view, this one.

Will you miss the sky, d'you think?

She turns back to the bed, her hand to her mouth.

Beat.

She goes slowly back to the bed and lifts the sheet to look at the body's face.

Oh, you've been– You're all red, round your eyes.

She puts the sheet back, and then thinks for a moment before sitting on the side of the bed.

Well I can't clean up now, can I? Least you didn't sick up on yourself, quite tidy really.

She reaches for the corpse's hand and holds it in her lap.

There you go.

Cold hands.

She looks intently at the back of the corpse's hand.

How old d'you have to be before you get the brown spots?

Pause. She goes to the end of the bed, lifts the sheet from the corpse's feet and looks at them. She touches the top of one of them lightly, then looks at the door. She sits back, thinking.

You know what gets me? Why wouldn't you go somewhere really good? Cause you're not going to have to pay for it next morning, are you? Why wouldn't you book into somewhere really posh, the Ritz or the Hilton or something, that's what I'd do. Get a bus to London, new credit card cause you'll not be around to pay the bill, will you? See a show. Have a nice long jacuzzi and then fall asleep forever but– But least it's a nice four-poster, Egyptian cotton. Chocolate on the pillow. Not a hotel on a bloody roundabout in this bloody shithole, nice plants in the lobby but if there's chocolate on the pillow means I didn't clean your room before you checked in. And it might not be chocolate…

AMY looks over at the tea-tray on the dressing table. She goes to it and picks up the tea cup.

Had a cup of tea, at least.

I'd like to do that. Something mad. Not. Not top myself but– Go somewhere. Far away in a fast car.

She looks back at the tray.

Didn't touch the shortbreads, I'm not surprised.

AMY looks out of the window.

Why would you not– Why wouldn't you think there was something *better* coming for you?

Like a person to come and drive you away, out of your life or.

Or something. You could wait for.

Most days all I want at the end of it's a sit down. A walk in the park even. Someone who wet shaves and likes buying me stuff and isn't a bastard like my dad. Someone to talk to.

She looks over at the corpse.

That's not dead.

Just cause you found a body you lost all your *hope*? That's it? What the bloody hell's going to happen to me, then?

AMY sighs. She moves back to the bed and sits on the end. She takes the corpse's foot in both her hands and looks at it. She rubs her hands over the foot slowly and then massages it, tentatively at first then with more confidence.

After a few moments she puts the foot down.

I think I will get the boot this time.

She picks up the other foot and massages it as she speaks.

You weren't to know.

They don't think I did it, not real– although I did get questioned last time cause they found my fingerprints on the bottle next to the bed, got in trouble for what was it, disturbing a crime scene– Manager says I'm the angel of death. Don't know why it's always me.

I mean, I do– I do think there's something wrong with me, there must–

She looks away, close to tears, then smiles.

Why can't the thing that makes me different be a nice

thing? Special cause I'm I don't know pretty or something. Someone people'd want to look after.

Stupid cow.

Beat.

I should go then. Go tell them. Not good to leave it too long.

She looks at the bed.

I hope you have a nice time. I don't believe in God, really, which is a shame in this type of situation, but–

AMY leaves the room, feigning hurry.

Fade.

SCENE 2

Monday afternoon, mid-December, heavy rain.

The reception area at Green Door Self-Storage. It's very brightly/ artificially lit, bright colours, lots of green. A service counter with a computer behind it. A rack of padlocks and packaging materials (parcel tape, rolls of bubble wrap, flat-packed boxes) stands to the side.

JIM stands behind the counter, surveying the area. He's wearing a checked shirt and khaki trousers – the boss, but not a suit. He goes round to the front of the counter and looks at a printed notice sellotaped to it: 'This weeks offer: sign up for 7 weeks storage, get the 8th for FREE'.

He frowns, takes the poster down and adds apostrophes with a black marker, then sticks it back up: 'This week's offer: sign up for 7 weeks' storage, get the 8th for FREE'.

He goes to sit behind the counter and straightens the boxes of leaflets standing on it. He takes out a glossy catalogue and reads.

The door opens from the car park and JIM puts his catalogue behind the counter, out of sight.

ELAINE and RAY enter, dripping with rain. ELAINE is mid-story, RAY is listening. She is smartly dressed under her raincoat, has made an effort. RAY wears the Green Door Self-Storage uniform – green dungarees and baseball cap.

ELAINE: …so I'm trying not to panic, but I'm starting to panic, and I'm thinking well I'd better ring Sky. But the way you ring them is you bring the number up on the screen and I can't get any of these buttons to work so I'm stuffed basically… Hi Jim.

JIM: Everything alright?

ELAINE: Ye-es. Yes.

JIM: You sure?

ELAINE: Thought I'd pop in and say hello. (*Taking her raincoat off.*) Miserable out there, found this one out in it, pushing trolleys around, silly boy.

JIM: I asked him / to–

ELAINE sits on a high stool in front of the counter, her legs crossed.

ELAINE: I said you'd want him to stop now it's siling down.

JIM: You just popped in to–

ELAINE: I missed you, gorgeous.

ELAINE mimes a kiss towards JIM, then turns back to RAY who leans awkwardly on the end of the counter, listening to her. JIM goes back to reading.

(*To RAY.*) …anyway, I have to ransack the house and I finally find the number to call and before she's even even asked my account number or code or anything I'm going 'I can't get my TV to work, it's just not working, I can't get it to work'. So the girl on the other end she's got this everso calm voice and she's saying 'Alright, calm down, OK, calm down' and I calm down and she's going 'Now what can you see?' and I tell her and she asks me if the light's on on the remote and I say 'Yes, yes but it's red and I can't get it to go green' so she goes 'OK, this is what I want you to do – go to the Skybox–' You got one of these, Ray?

RAY: Er. Yeah.

ELAINE: Cause it's all a bit of a mystery to me this little box, only the kids know how to work it so now they're off at college– anyway, she says she wants me to find the, the power cable, which I do and she says 'OK, I want you to unplug it'. And I'm / thinking–

JIM: Hang on to your socks, Ray, punchline's coming.

ELAINE: Shut up. I'm. Jim. (*Back to RAY.*) I'm thinking that sounds a bit drastic so I say 'God, are you sure' and she's really firm saying 'Yes – unplug it'. So I unplug it and she tells me we have to leave it alone. For a minute.

So we sit there on the phone in silence for a whole minute – feels like forever, you know how a minute's silence feels–

123

JIM: Never get one with you…

ELAINE: You know what I– Jim. You know what I mean, Ray?

RAY: Um, yeah.

ELAINE: Cause you can just hear the other person breathing, if I was her I'd be typing or something just to make some noise, but she doesn't she just sits there and I'm sitting on the floor this end with the plug in my hand and I've never been more *aware* of myself. I'm getting more and more panicky and she says she says 'You still there' and I say 'yes' and then we're back to feeling out the length of this minute and then finally – finally finally finally – we get to 60 seconds and she says 'OK, here's what I want you to do. I want you to–

ELAINE pauses momentarily for effect. JIM doesn't look up from his reading.

JIM: Plug it back in again.

ELAINE: Plug it back in again!

RAY laughs. Briefly.

Thanks.

JIM: No, thank you. Suddenly my day seems all productive and worthwhile.

ELAINE: Well the point *is*, the point is it made me think I should probably get out a bit. Pop in and see you at work sometimes…

JIM: God help us. Don't stand there, Ray, she'll start another.

RAY: Right. Um, can I–

ELAINE: Anyway it's broken again now so–

JIM: Fill that rack, yeah…

RAY: Yeah.

JIM: …while I put my wife back in her box.

ELAINE: What you doing's so important, then?

JIM: Reading.

ELAINE: Yeah, what?

ELAINE leans over the counter trying to see what JIM is doing. He moves it so that she can't see.

JIM: Work, alright?

RAY: What d'you think, though?

ELAINE leans over to try to have another look.

JIM: Oy. (*To RAY.*) Bout what?

RAY: Y'know…

JIM: Oh. Yep, funny smell.

ELAINE: What's this?

RAY: Really funny.

JIM: Not *really* funny, no.

RAY: Don't you think?

JIM: Not really, no.

RAY: You don't think we should have a look?

JIM: Need more reason than a funny smell to go busting stuff open, dipstick.

ELAINE: Bust what open?

JIM: Bit of a funny smell coming off one of the units / that's all.

RAY: Very funny smell.

JIM: Ray.

RAY: Like–

ELAINE: Like what?

RAY: Nothing. Funny.

JIM: I'll give the guy a call.

RAY: You see the size of the padlock?

JIM: No accounting for people, paranoia... I'll give him a call.

JIM looks at RAY.

RAY: Right. Yeah.

RAY goes out.

JIM: Put him in charge of security accessories. Think I'd given him a badge and a gun, the way he's– Did you have to go on about Sky?

ELAINE: He laughed.

JIM: Not the point.

ELAINE: You shouldn't call him dipstick, he's got no confidence already–

JIM: Do yourself down, sounds like you sit at home all day with your feet up.

ELAINE: I pretty much do, love, now the boys are gone...

JIM: Got to call this bloke.

ELAINE: Came in cause I missed you.

JIM: Right.

ELAINE: Sorry.

Beat. RAY comes back in, a box of padlocks in his hand. Sees there's an atmosphere.

RAY: Sorry, I–

JIM: No, no. You get on.

RAY: Right. Boss–

ELAINE: D'you ask him to call you boss?

JIM: Just a joke, office joke.

ELAINE: You can call him Jim, you know.

JIM: He knows.

ELAINE: I call him fathead sometimes, but it's affectionate, isn't it?

RAY: Right.

RAY goes over to the display rack and puts the box of padlocks down by it. He looks at the box, lost in thought.

ELAINE rummages in her bag.

ELAINE: Here – I brought you something. Stopped off to get you a bacon sarnie. Extra red sauce.

She hands JIM a sandwich in a paper bag, then rummages again and pulls out another.

JIM: It's three in the afternoon.

ELAINE: I know, but– I don't know. Shouldn't watch the news, really. Made me want to come see you, bring you something. Don't have to eat it.

JIM: You watched the news?

ELAINE: I do sometimes. Not much else on cause of them capturing um– Bacon sarnie, Ray?

RAY: Oh. Cheers.

ELAINE hands RAY the second paper bag.

JIM: Capturing who?

ELAINE: Hussein.

JIM: Saddam?

ELAINE: Yep.

JIM: Hussein's his first name, they do it the other way / round.

ELAINE: Found him hiding in a hole. I didn't get you any red
sauce, Ray, didn't know if you liked it.

RAY: Ah thanks.

JIM: Where?

RAY: I do like it. Red sauce.

ELAINE: Remember next time.

RAY: Got some in the kitchen…

JIM: A hole where?

RAY goes out.

ELAINE: Desert somewhere. Little hole in the ground, like a
little mole or something.

You going to call that man, then?

JIM: You've just given me a bacon sarnie, I'm not doing
anything.

JIM eats his sandwich.

ELAINE: Imagine being the soldier walking up to that hole
and not knowing two minutes later you'd have saved the
western world. Imagine that.

JIM: Uh-huh.

ELAINE: Like when the doorbell's rung – that bit where
you're walking to the door and you don't know who it is
yet.

Ketchup on your face, love.

Funny, though. Doesn't look like he'd kill millions of
people.

JIM: (*Eating.*) Wha?

ELAINE: Remember thinking that last time, always think he's
got a really kind face.

JIM: He's a dictator.

ELAINE: Doesn't look it, though, does he?

JIM: I think they've a fair bit of evidence, it's not difficult.

ELAINE: I know, but. Like the time before, when he was on telly with all the little kids.

JIM: Hostages.

ELAINE: Seemed really nice, patting them all on the head. Like an uncle.

RAY comes back in. Takes a knife from his pocket and starts to open the box of padlocks with one hand, his sandwich (now oozing ketchup) in the other.

RAY: Did you call him, boss? That bloke.

JIM: Not yet. After I've eaten this.

RAY looks at ELAINE. ELAINE looks at JIM.

Chuffing hell. Do it now, then.

JIM goes into the office behind the counter.

ELAINE: Alright Ray?

RAY: Yeah. Mrs–

ELAINE: Elaine. Mrs Boss if you like. Chief of padlocks, eh?

RAY: Yeah.

ELAINE: Well done.

RAY: Thanks, I– Thanks.

ELAINE: You'll do well, be good at that.

ELAINE leans over the counter.

What's this he's reading then?

She picks up a catalogue and looks at it.

LAURA WADE

> Golden Moments. Give the gift of an exciting day out.
> Bloody hell. Have you seen this, Ray?

RAY: Yeah. I like the–

ELAINE: God the things you can do – ballooning, bungee
jumping, fly a fighter plane, god listen to this – Fly a MIG
fighter plane…

RAY: Yeah.

ELAINE: …Fly to Moscow day 1 and spend the day relaxing
and sightseeing. Day 2 you are fully briefed and trained
for your thirty minute flying experience. Thirty minutes!
Seems a long way to go for half an hour of fun, doesn't it?

RAY: Yeah.

She flicks through further.

ELAINE: Oh, there we are, Day at a Health Spa, that's it. Ray,
if he's getting one of these for me it's the health spa, not the
fighter jet, alright?

RAY: Bungee jump, maybe.

ELAINE: Rather stick pins in my eyes. You could, though,
young enough…

RAY: Nah. Don't really–

ELAINE is looking over the counter again.

ELAINE: Ooh, there's chocolates here.

*She pulls out a box of Celebrations, two thirds full. Closes her eyes
and puts her hand in. Pulls out a chocolate and looks at it.*

Pff. Malteser.

She eats it anyway.

Chocolate, Ray?

*RAY is about to take one when JIM comes back in. ELAINE holds
the box out of sight.*

RAY: Yeah?

JIM: No answer. Try later.

RAY goes back to the padlock rack. ELAINE and JIM stare out at the car park.

ELAINE: Still raining, then.

ELAINE leans over the counter to put the chocolate box back.

Bit quiet, isn't it?

JIM: Afternoon. Low period.

ELAINE: So bloody quiet in the house. Empty nest.

JIM: Danny's back tomorrow.

ELAINE: He's not actually.

JIM: Oh.

ELAINE: Couple of parties and things he wants to go to next week, so– Well it's more exciting there than being with us old sods, isn't it? Understandable he'd want to stay, probably all stay a bit after the end of term, promised he'd be back well before Christmas day.

JIM: When?

ELAINE: Twenty-third. Same as Mark. Get them both a few days at least.

They look out at the car park.

Understandable, isn't it?

Beat.

Doesn't seem fair.

JIM: No.

RAY is intent on the padlock rack. JIM looks over and sees that he's not looking, then leans over the counter and kisses ELAINE on the cheek.

ELAINE smiles, still looking out.

RAY is staring at a padlock in his hand. He makes a decision and turns to JIM.

RAY: What was his name?

JIM: What?

RAY: B Sixteen.

JIM looks at the computer.

JIM: Ben Elliott. You did the form, it says here.

RAY: Ben Elliott. What's he look like?

JIM: I dunno Ray, you served him, we don't put a description on.

RAY: Did he have a dog?

ELAINE: You think he's put a dog in there?

RAY: No, just– Nothing.

JIM: Ray?

RAY: (*To ELAINE.*) Can't stash something alive, says in the storage agreement. Nothing that'll decompose. (*To JIM.*) Remember the kebab van?

JIM: Yeah.

ELAINE: A kebab van?

RAY: Go on, you tell it better than me.

JIM: Man has kebab van, I've told you this story–

ELAINE: No, tell me.

JIM: Well he buys a job lot of those elephant leg things–

RAY: Doner kebab.

JIM: – and he can't fit them in his van so he hires a unit, doesn't tell us what he's putting in and it's a plain enough box, it's not like it's from a legitimate supplier. Then his van gets stolen and he forgets all about these bloody kebabs, goes back to live with his mum in Wigan. First we know about it, four weeks later, the smell gets you every time you go–

RAY: Cause that unit's just there, just behind the office–

JIM: Am I telling this or–

RAY: Sorry.

JIM: So I think it's a dead bird on the roof for a while, didn't do anything about it. Don't realise it's A Five till the maggots start crawling under the door.

ELAINE: Oh my god.

RAY: Nasty.

ELAINE: What happened?

JIM: Tried to call but he'd naffed off to Wigan so– Then there's women coming in here complaining, you know, not fair on the other customers. Broke the door in. I've definitely told you this.

ELAINE: Didn't he have a padlock?

JIM: You've got to have some way of getting into the units yourself, could be anything.

RAY: Firearms, drugs, explosives...

JIM: Got a responsibility.

ELAINE: How'd you do it, then?

JIM: Trade secret.

RAY: Won't tell me, either.

JIM: And if I'm not telling dipstick I'm not telling you.

RAY: B Sixteen smells a bit like that, though, doesn't it?

LAURA WADE

ELAINE: Go on, have a look if you can get in…

JIM: What about this dog, then?

RAY: Just– When he came in it was– Funny I remember it
but– One of them really really hot days. You know we had
that weird heatwave, late September?

JIM: Yes.

RAY: Came in with his dog and I said he couldn't bring it in
here–

ELAINE: Why can't you bring a dog in?

JIM: Chew the bubble wrap, gets messy.

RAY: Well I tell him he can't bring it in, and he um he gets a
bit shirty, says he can't leave her in the car, she'll get hot
and die, hadn't I seen the advert… But he backs down after
a second, bloke's sweating like a pig–

ELAINE: How old?

RAY: Bout my age, bit older? Gives in and ties the dog up
outside, and you should have heard the racket it made
waiting for him…

ELAINE: Probably a young one.

RAY: Made this this horrible whining noise, goes right through
you – kind of noise gets you here.

ELAINE: Did you see what he put in?

JIM: Oy, my interrogation, thank you. (*To RAY.*) Did you?

RAY: Not properly. Some kind of big box, I think, had it on
a trolley all wrapped in plastic, tape all over it. Didn't
see properly cause the dog was there, making the noise
so– Thought it might have got run over or something so I
went out, and it's just turning round and round on the spot,
like it's mental.

ELAINE: So what d'you do? (*To JIM.*) Sorry.

RAY: Well I go in and look for him, and he's doing his padlock up. Yeah, cause I remember he jumped when I. And he looked like he was listening dead hard to what I was saying he was like frowning and nodding loads and sweat on his forehead but we all did that week, and he's just moved this fuckoff big box...

JIM: Yes–

RAY: Yeah so I said I was worried the dog'd do itself an injury, choke itself on the lead or something and then he nods and went a bit white and rushed off.

JIM: OK. And did he look in any way like he might be the kind of bloke runs a kebab van?

RAY: No.

JIM: Or any other kind of perishable foodstuff he might have had in there?

RAY: He was a bit posh actually. Rugby shirt.

JIM: Right.

RAY: But I noticed he had a Cruiser.

ELAINE: What's a Cruiser?

RAY: Big fuckoff padlock. Fort Knox of security accessories.

ELAINE: So he's hiding something.

RAY: I reckon.

ELAINE: Jim, don't you think– I mean if Ray thinks so, he's got the specialist knowledge on padlocks...

JIM: He started padlocks on Monday.

ELAINE: Think you should look.

JIM: Think you should go home.

ELAINE: But what if it's something–

JIM: (*To RAY.*) You wait to mention it now, after–

RAY: I know, but– I mean, yeah, he looked a bit shifty but I thought he was just in a piss about the dog, and it– I can't, I mean, it was bastard hot that week, everyone's acting a bit funny, you know?

ELAINE: He's right, it was a bit funny, wasn't it?

JIM: Would you get off home, please?

ELAINE: What if Health and Safety come in, eh, and it turns out you've got a dead dog or something and you chose not to do anything?

RAY: See, I thought about saying something, but then I forgot and I–

ELAINE: They'd close you down.

RAY: Didn't think about it till the smell.

JIM: Right.

RAY: I just remembered it now, so–

ELAINE: D'you have to call the police?

JIM: After I've had a look. RSPCA with any luck.

ELAINE: I think you should. Have a look.

RAY: I'll do it.

JIM: Bollocks will you.

RAY: Thing is–

JIM: What?

RAY: I think I did see a maggot, think I might have stepped on one.

JIM: Bloody hell.

ELAINE: Got a responsibility, haven't you, don't want complaints. Go on, I'll bugger off home if you have a look first. Back in my box.

JIM: Ray, watch the counter.

JIM looks out to the carpark.

You'll go even if it's still raining?

ELAINE: Yep.

JIM: Back in a minute, then.

He goes.

ELAINE: See, that's love for you, anything to get rid of me. You alright?

RAY is looking in the direction JIM went off.

RAY: Yeah, just–

ELAINE: I'd have done the same–

RAY: Yeah, I just–

ELAINE leans over the counter and pulls out the box of Celebrations.

ELAINE: Here, have a chocolate. I won't tell.

RAY goes to take one, ELAINE pulls the box away.

No-no, no choosing – close your eyes and stick your hand in.

RAY does so.

Fade.

SCENE 3

Sunday lunchtime, late September, the hottest day in a freak heatwave. Outside, a car alarm goes off sporadically.

The kitchen of KATE's house. KATE is at the kitchen table, talking on the phone. She wears shorts and a t-shirt, and a baseball cap. There is a laptop computer on the table in front of her.

A dog barks close by.

KATE: Cameron, will you–

> (*Into phone.*) No, it's fine. When you've finished, yeah? Cam– Yeah, finish your lunch– No, just– Something to tell you, just– No, nothing to worry about – Yeah, yeah, when you've finished. Get Dad to wash up. OK. Yeah, Mum, eat your lunch. OK. Bye.

> *KATE hangs up. She wipes sweat off her face and blows on it with her bottom lip sticking out. She looks at the laptop screen, frowning.*

> *The dog barks again.*

Shut up, dogshit.

> *A pause. Then more barking.*

Cameron, will you–

> *Still barking.*

Fuck's sake–

> *KATE leaves the kitchen.*

> (*Off.*) Will you *shut* (*The dog yelps.*) the *fuck* (*Another yelp.*) up!

> *Silence. KATE returns, limping slightly. She sits down and clutches her foot in pain, then pulls off a broken toenail.*

> (*Under her breath.*) Bitch.

> *She looks at the computer then goes back to it and types furiously.*

BEN comes into the kitchen and leans on the work surface. He also wears shorts and a t-shirt. He has a pore-cleansing strip on his nose.

KATE looks at BEN. He points at his nose.

BEN: Chinatown.

KATE: What?

BEN: Chinatown. Jack Nicholson.

KATE: That's a plaster isn't it?

BEN: Have you seen it?

KATE: Before your bollocks dropped, love.

A look.

BEN: What?

KATE: You should ask before you use my bath stuff.

BEN: I didn't think you'd–

KATE: Looks a bit like biting the hand that takes you on holiday / that's all.

BEN: OK.

KATE: Quite expensive those.

BEN: I'll get some more.

KATE: Yeah, with what?

BEN: How much are they?

KATE: I don't know, about a quid each / or something.

BEN: Well, fuck's sake, I'll give you a quid.

KATE: No, it doesn't– I'm just / fucked off.

BEN: Sorry.

BEN sits at the table, opposite KATE.

You OK?

KATE: Busy.

BEN: I mean about yesterday. The girl.

KATE: I'm fine.

BEN: D'you want coffee, tea?

KATE: I'm not traumatised, I'm just fucked off.

BEN: OK. Just thought you might like a coffee, I thought I'd make you one, would you like a coffee?

KATE: You don't ha– OK.

BEN: Cool.

BEN switches the kettle on.

Fucking hot, isn't it?

KATE: Just ask next time, yeah?

BEN: Sorry, yeah.

KATE: Don't have time to go to Boots this week.

BEN: I didn't use the last one, I wouldn't do that.

KATE: God, give him a medal.

BEN: Would you prefer a Coke, actually? Or water, juice?

KATE: Coffee.

BEN: OK.

KATE: *Fucksticks.*

BEN: What?

KATE: Stupid fucking– *Ngh!* All of yesterday lost at the fucking police station, now the cunting thing's crashed on me–

BEN: Switch it off and on again it'll be–

KATE hits the laptop keyboard with her fist.

KATE: Fuck!

BEN: Kate–

KATE: Didn't fucking save it, did I?

BEN: What can I do, can I help you?

KATE: I'm surrounded by fucking–

BEN: Can I help?

KATE: What the fuck help d'you think you could be?

BEN: I don't know, I–

KATE: Keep that fucking animal out of my face, you can do that.

BEN: Sure.

BEN spoons instant coffee into a mug and pours water onto it, then stirs and hands it to KATE.

Why's she in her basket?

KATE: I don't know.

KATE takes a sip of her coffee and makes a face.

BEN: Kate?

KATE: Cause she's tired, cause she's hot? Everyone's hot, it's so hot outside all you can hear is screaming…

BEN: Did you kick her?

KATE: …everything's melting, that car alarm keeps going off and it's not cause anyone's touched it, just the air's so heavy, all the kids shrieking, just think give them a drink of water for fuck's–

BEN: Did you kick her?

KATE: She does that, she goes and hides in her basket, looks all wounded, trying to make you think I / kicked–

BEN: Did you kick her?

KATE: No.

BEN: OK. Controlled the impulse.

KATE stands up and puts three more spoonfuls of instant coffee into her mug.

KATE: Stop doing the patient voice, makes you sound like a wanker.

BEN: Thought you were going to try having two spoons, cut down a bit.

KATE: Just as much caffeine in tea.

BEN: I don't have three teabags.

KATE: I didn't sleep it's not– Trying to run a business here. Whole day yesterday shot to shit cause of your stupid mutt. Barking for a walk at nine o'clock on a fucking Saturday.

BEN: I do appreciate it. You walking her, it's–

KATE: Best way to shut her up, isn't it? Glad you managed to sleep through it.

BEN: Sorry.

KATE: *Fucking* thing.

BEN: Can you stop shouting at the / computer–

KATE: What?

BEN: It's alarming, it–

KATE: Won't even let me switch off... *Cunt.*

BEN: Kate.

KATE subsides a little.

Look, I'm sorry about– I'm sorry you ended up walking her, I'm sorry you–

KATE: No, it's fine. Love talking to the police on my day off. Would you leave me / alone?

BEN: Well that's what I came down to say, so–

KATE puts her head in her hands.

Are you OK?

KATE: Just shitloads to do. Massive stack of CVs, candidates with shit-hot qualifications and no social skills that no-one's going to hire, then the forecast for the bank and–

Hate Sundays, make you feel all–

KATE spoons three sugars into her coffee and stirs it. Then she leans across the table and holds the hot spoon from her coffee on BEN's arm.

BEN flinches, but doesn't say anything.

I really hated you last night.

KATE sits back in her chair.

BEN: It was hot. You couldn't sleep either.

KATE: You kept pushing all the blankets over. You were breathing.

BEN: Would you like me to / stop?

KATE: You were breathing *loudly.*

BEN: You were breathing / loudly.

KATE: Only when I was fucked off with you.

BEN puts a hand to his arm.

BEN: That really hurt.

KATE shrugs.

You kept putting the light on…

KATE: See the clock. Have to know the time, how long you're not sleeping for.

BEN: We always used to–

KATE: What?

BEN: When we couldn't sleep. We'd put the light on and chat for a bit.

KATE: Yeah.

BEN: Why don't we do that anymore? We'd sit up and play games, talk about crap, make love even.

KATE: 'Make love'.

BEN: Last night we just lay there getting pissed off with each other.

KATE: When it's hot, isn't it?

BEN: Yeah.

KATE: Makes you irritable.

BEN: Going to be like this all week, they said. Hottest September on record.

BEN peels his shirt off and sniffs it, then pulls a face. Puts it into the washing machine. KATE looks at him. His torso is covered with red marks and bruises.

KATE: You–

BEN: You. Last night.

KATE: That bad?

BEN: You were there.

Get Cameron fed…

BEN takes out a dog bowl and a tin of food. He starts decanting food from the tin with a fork. KATE watches him. After a few moments BEN notices her looking at him.

Babe, it's fine.

BEN comes over and leans down to kiss her. KATE recoils.

What?

KATE: Dog fork. Stinks.

BEN laughs. Puts the fork down on the surface and comes back towards KATE.

I don't want to kiss you it fucking stinks.

BEN goes back to the dog food, continues decanting it, then mashes it with the fork.

D'you have to–

BEN: What?

KATE: You couldn't put your shirt back on, or–

BEN: Too hot.

KATE: OK.

BEN: It's fine in the winter, isn't it, can just cover it all up.

KATE: We could get you summer shirts....

BEN: You could stop.

KATE: I'm–

BEN: I know.

KATE looks at him.

Yeah.

She takes her baseball cap off, runs her hands through her hair.

KATE: Ben, last night...

BEN: Yeah?

KATE: What was it about? I– I can't remember. What it was about.

BEN: The girl under the bush, wasn't it? I think that's what precipitated / it.

KATE: Fuck you it wasn't that. Forget it, I've got to get this–

Shit, Ben, I'm so fucking angry. I'm so fucking fucking angry just *fuck* and I don't know–

And after I'm angry I'm just fucking tired, right now I'm…

Beat.

BEN: Hot.

KATE: I don't have time for this, you know?

BEN: Yeah.

KATE: Like, the minute I saw her I was I was like 'shit, how long is this going to fuck things up for?'

BEN: How d'you mean?

KATE: Like– like you know how when something happens and it it comes in the middle of everything and you're trying to, to *feel* to feel the length of it–

BEN: The length of–

KATE: Like how long it's going to disrupt you for…

BEN: OK.

KATE: …and how long you're *expected* to be disrupted for / like–

BEN: I don't–

KATE: Like, grandma's died, so I guess I'll be off work a couple of days, sad for a few weeks, forget about it by two months– But you've got this um, this *dismay* because you know it's got to happen and it buggers up everything, stuff you were trying to get done, and without you having any warning, just everything disrupted and out the window….

BEN: And this was the first thing you thought–

KATE: No, I mean I–

BEN: After you felt sorry for her– You did / feel–

KATE: No, of course I– Of course I felt sorry for her I'm not fucking heartless, I didn't want her, whoever she is, to end up under a bush, *god*, but I didn't I didn't want it to be me and your stupid fucking dog that found her / either.

BEN: It's not Cameron's fault–

KATE: Forget it. / I've got to do this.

BEN: It's not just another reason for you to–

KATE: Ben shut up or I'll get angry. Put a shirt on. Something.

Cameron barks. BEN picks up a rugby shirt from the back of the chair.

BEN: Got that barbecue to go to later.

KATE: Cause the world needs another heat source right now.

KATE sees what BEN is wearing.

You'll be boiling in that.

BEN: You wanted me to put something / on–

KATE: Something that didn't make me feel bad.

BEN: If we go, will you be nice?

KATE: If you wear something / else–

BEN: I'll change before we go, I'm not going upstairs to get something / now–

KATE: Hold me.

Beat.

BEN: It's too hot.

KATE: Please.

He holds her. But it's not a hug, it's boxers holding each other as they pause mid-fight.

BEN: OK?

KATE: Yeah.

> *Cameron barks again.*

> Oh, for fuck's–

BEN: Shh. She just wants her food.

> *BEN puts his hands in the back of KATE's hair and kisses her, hard.*

> *After a moment, KATE pulls away.*

KATE: You're all sweaty.

BEN: So are you.

KATE: You stink.

BEN: You want to go upstairs?

KATE: Why?

BEN: We could shower.

KATE: I don't like sex standing up.

BEN: It doesn't have to be sex.

KATE: Last time I gave you a blowjob in the shower I nearly drowned.

BEN: Come on, it's Sunday afternoon, let's go back to bed. We could do the thing I was talking about…

KATE: Ben I've explained, it's just the wrong hole.

> *They laugh. BEN touches KATE's face. He melts.*

BEN: Your eyes…when you laugh…

> *They're about to kiss again when Cameron barks.*

KATE: Shut her up.

BEN: She wants walking.

KATE: She hates me.

BEN: Because you're a bitch to her.

KATE: I walked her yesterday, I tried and she still hates me. She hates that you fuck me and not her.

BEN: Kate, you can't act like a world-class cunt and then expect people / to–

KATE: Dogs–

BEN: People *or* dogs. You can't behave like that poor dead girl existed only to

The phone rings.

fuck up your weekend–

KATE picks up the phone. She holds eye contact with BEN as she speaks into it.

KATE: Hi Mum. Cause your number comes up on the– Caller Display, yeah. You finished lunch? Yeah, I – Yeah, pretty good. Found a dead body in the park yesterday then I've been getting some work done today and we're going to a barbecue ton– Yeah. Some girl under a bush. I don't know, eighteen, nineteen. Yeah. Walking Cameron. I do walk her some– No, not a prostitute, looked like a waitress or something, black skirt, white shirt, sensible shoes, you know? Didn't identify her yet, this was only yesterday, so– Police kept me for hours, statements and– It was on the news. I was 'a woman walking her dog in Newbold Park'. Wanted to call the channel and say 'It's not my fucking dog, it's his fucking dog, I only walked it cause I can't sleep through the Saturday morning barking festival...

How's Dad?

BEN picks up Cameron's dog food bowl and goes out.

Had her throat slit. I know. Really straight cut across. Something really fucking sharp. Hardly any blood, though, like it all went into the ground or her hair, hardly any on her shirt...

It was surreal.

I think surreal. Never know if I'm using that word right...

It's weird, it's details, things you keep seeing. Like I noticed I had dirt up my fingernails, just a second before, and I hoped the dog wasn't going to the bush to have a shit because then I'd have to pick it up in the bag and carry it to the next– And when I saw her I thought, well first I thought fuck you, dogshit, thanks for that, that's my day fucked, isn't it?

No, I did feel sorry for her. I just– there's loads to do with the company, and– I'm not overdoing it, this is– You have to work at the weekend when you run your own business. And now they want me back in tomorrow for more statements so that's half a day's work lost...

BEN comes back with blood on his hand. He looks at KATE.

So it was weird, anyway. Yeah.

BEN: Hang up.

Beat.

KATE: Mum– Mum, can I call you later in the week? Yeah, Ben needs me, I– OK. Love you too.

KATE hangs up and looks at BEN.

BEN: How hard d'you have to fucking kick her to draw blood?

KATE: I didn't–

BEN: Show me your shoes.

KATE: What?

BEN: Show me your shoes / the ones on your feet–

KATE: No, I'm not–

BEN lunges at KATE, a kind of rugby tackle in which she falls to the ground and BEN rips the flip-flops from her feet. He examines her toes, and the shoes.

BEN: So what's this red stuff, then, ketchup?

KATE: You didn't see me / do–

BEN: She's hiding in her basket, scared shitless and she's got a cut on her side, you've got blood under your toenails, it's not rocket, is it?

KATE doesn't say anything. Looks at the floor.

BEN pauses a moment then looks as if he will lash out at KATE with her shoe. Instead, he turns and aims a savage blow at the kitchen work surface.

KATE: What you doing?

BEN: Moral fucking high ground.

Another blow to the work surface.

I'm going to give her this as a fucking chew toy.

KATE gets up.

I think you should apologise.

Pause.

KATE: I'm sorry.

BEN: To Cameron.

KATE: She doesn't unders–

BEN: I want you on your knees in front of her.

KATE: Fine, OK.

BEN: On your knees.

KATE: Yeah.

BEN: Now, before I walk her, if she's up to–

KATE: Fuck's sake.

KATE moves to leave.

Do I have to bark or will English do?

BEN: She'll understand.

KATE goes out. BEN opens a drawer, takes out the dog lead. A moment.

You on your knees in there?

KATE comes back in. Goes towards the laptop.

KATE: This is fucking–

BEN: What?

KATE: Fucking ridiculous I'm not apologising to the bloody *dog*–

KATE laughs.

Idiot.

She looks at him, sees he's glaring at her.

Look, I'm sorry, OK, I got– Babe, come here…

She motions for him to come closer to her, to lean down to kiss her. As he's leaning in she rips the pore strip off his nose, laughing.

BEN: Ow–

KATE: You can't stand there and say things with that on, you look like a twat.

She examines the strip.

Oh my god, look at this, fucking disgusting like you ooze this kind of–

BEN grabs KATE by her hair, twists his hand into the back of it and pulls her up until she's standing.

Ow, fuck, Ben–

BEN: Why d'you have to be so fucking–

KATE: I–

BEN: How did I end up with such a fucking–

KATE: Ben–

BEN: What, does it, does this hurt?

KATE: Yes.

BEN: Does it hurt like your fucking fingernails, like boiling water, like the way you look at me / when you're–

KATE: I don't / know.

BEN: No, you don't know, you don't fucking know.

KATE: OK, I–

BEN: You've got to fucking stop, Kate. D'you have any idea what this fucking *does*? I never fucking heal my bruises have got bruises on them I'm always–

KATE: Leave if you–

BEN: What?

KATE: You can–

BEN: What?

KATE: Leave if you–

BEN: I can't fucking–

KATE: Fucking *leave*–

> *KATE grabs her coffee cup from the table and hurls it at the wall.*

BEN: I can't I can't you know I fucking can't I haven't got *anything* I'm fucking staying but–

KATE: Let me go–

BEN: But you're making it *really* / difficult to–

KATE: Fuck you–

BEN: If you push me, if you really push me, you know I'm stronger. I could snap you in two if I wanted to and I don't want to I really don't want to but this is no way to *live*, Kate…

KATE flails, tries to kick him.

…and you try and say it's the girl, it's because of the girl, it's not the girl you're always like this and it's got to fucking *stop*.

He shakes her hard.

KATE: Stop!

He stops shaking her, but keeps hold.

BEN: Are we going to stop or carry on?

KATE: Stop.

BEN: We're choosing now, we're going to stop this, yeah?

KATE: Yeah.

BEN: We're going to be like normal people, go out for dinner and shit, yeah?

KATE: Yeah.

BEN: See our friends like normal fucking people.

KATE: Yeah.

BEN: OK.

BEN releases KATE's hair. KATE looks at the floor.

Look at me.

KATE looks up at him.

You're a fucking bitch but I / love you.

KATE: You've got hair in your hand.

BEN looks down at his hand – there's a clump of hair in it.

KATE puts her hand to the back of her head.

You pulled a whole clump out.

BEN: That's what it feels like.

KATE: Fuck that hurt.

BEN: This is for you to learn.

Go and apologise to Cameron.

KATE: What– I backed / down for–

BEN: Learn, Kate.

KATE moves away.

KATE: OK.

She frowns.

Fuckit Ben–

Her fists clench and she goes back to BEN and punches him squarely in the back. He reels.

BEN: Fucking –

KATE: God all-fucking mighty you're so full of shit. I'm not apologising to your fucking dog.

BEN: You said we were going to–

KATE: Fuck you.

KATE goes out. BEN picks up the dog lead, whips it fiercely at the table, then looks at it in his hand. Looks after KATE.

BEN: Fine.

He follows her out, twisting the dog lead in his hand.

Fade.

SCENE 4

Tuesday evening, mid-January, dark already, getting cold.

The garage at JIM's house. JIM sits cross-legged on the floor, carefully removing the screws from a brass door handle. Beside him, underneath a camping groundsheet, is a pile of doors.

ELAINE calls from inside the house.

ELAINE: I'm home, love.

> *She enters the doorway to the garage. She is wearing Green Door Self-Storage dungarees underneath her outdoor coat.*
>
> *JIM doesn't look up, but continues with the handle.*

Born in a barn?

JIM: What?

ELAINE: Doesn't– How you feeling, good day?

JIM: Alright.

ELAINE: OK well alright's better than yesterday–

JIM: Not great.

ELAINE: OK. But– Working towards great, that's the thing, isn't it?

JIM: Uh-huh.

ELAINE: Trying.

JIM: Yep.

> *JIM stops. Puts the handle down. Looks up at ELAINE. She's taking her coat off.*

Look at you.

ELAINE: Thought I'd– you know, try and look like the rest. Not the boss-lady or anything, cause I keep having to ask how to do things so that wouldn't work...

What d'you think?

JIM: Yeah. Suits you.

ELAINE: Great.

JIM frowns.

No, you're right, that's usually the right answer. Just–
(*Exhales.*) Need a bath, my feet hate me for being in flat
shoes all day…

I picked up the prescription…

ELAINE fumbles in her bag and pulls out a pharmacy packet.

JIM: Ta.

*JIM takes the bottle and looks at the label. He turns the lid of
the bottle and the safety catch clicks.*

ELAINE: Here–

*ELAINE takes the bottle and unscrews it successfully. She hands
it back to JIM.*

JIM: Not going to sleep yet, am I?

ELAINE: Screw it back on then. What you doing?

JIM: Fixing things.

ELAINE: Jim the front door was wide open, didn't you–

ELAINE smiles.

D'you remember, with Danny?

'Yes, dad, I *was* born in a barn, cause I'm Jesus'.
Remember?

Should keep it closed though, really. Security.

Did the boys ring?

JIM: No.

ELAINE: No. Well, only two weeks since they were here, wasn't it? Spect they will soon. Check up on you.

JIM doesn't reply.

I brought Ray back. Can he come in and see you?

JIM: You've got him waiting outside?

ELAINE: No– he's–

JIM: Queuing.

ELAINE: He's in the kitchen. I wanted to check with you first.

JIM: Out in the waiting room...

ELAINE: Thought you might like a bit of– you know, not just me. Can I get him?

JIM shrugs.

OK.

ELAINE goes back into the house through the doorway. A moment later she comes back to the doorframe and stands in it, frowning. She runs a hand over where the hinges used to be attached.

You've taken the door off.

JIM: Yep.

ELAINE: Are you, what, fixing it?

JIM: Open plan. Nicer without the door.

ELAINE: OK.

Beat.

What if, what about when I'm in there cooking and I want my music on, you're in here wanting peace and quiet?

OK.

ELAINE goes back into the house. JIM scratches his head, then rubs the palms of his hands on his forehead. He puts a finger to one nostril and blows really hard, then does the same on the other side. He then blows hard down both nostrils, concentrating.

ELAINE comes back into the doorway.

You've taken all the doors off.

JIM: Yep.

ELAINE: What've you–

JIM pulls the groundsheet off the pile of doors. There are nine.

How long did that take you?

JIM: Bout ten minutes each.

ELAINE: But wh– OK.

Ray?

RAY appears in the doorway.

RAY: Alright Boss?

JIM nods. RAY steps into the garage.

ELAINE: He's taken all the doors off.

RAY: Yeah, what d'you use?

JIM: Electric screwdriver.

RAY: Yeah, Black & Decker?

JIM: Bosch.

RAY: I'm getting a DeWalt next week. Upgrading.

ELAINE: Ten minutes per door. Take me hours.

RAY: Nah, when you've got the right tools it–

JIM looks at RAY. An uncomfortable pause.

ELAINE: We heard this thing on the radio this morning, this story, what was it, Ray?

RAY: Um–

ELAINE: The one about the man–

RAY: Yeah, there's this man–

ELAINE: With the lifts–

RAY: Oh, yeah, this– this bloke ran a company made lifts–

ELAINE: For office buildings and things.

RAY: Yeah and he was forty and he suddenly got, um, claustrophobia.

ELAINE: And vertigo.

RAY: So he couldn't, you know, he couldn't go inside his lifts anymore. And the company was going to go bust if he didn't sort it out so he got um, he got–

ELAINE: Therapy.

RAY: Yeah. And he got better.

ELAINE: And now they even make glass lifts. And we thought–

RAY: Boss, we've eaten all your chocolates. She found your stash.

ELAINE: Ray–

RAY: Sorry.

ELAINE: I'm going to– I'll be inside, OK?

RAY: Was that alright?

ELAINE: Yes.

ELAINE goes out. RAY stands awkwardly looking at JIM. JIM holds the pill bottle and clicks the cap round and round.

JIM: It true that story?

RAY: Yeh. I mean I– I didn't hear it myself, in and out the office like a bull in a cuckoo clock... What's that?

JIM: Nothing.

JIM puts the pill bottle to one side.

Going all right, customers in?

RAY: Yeah, good few. For– Y'know, for January.

JIM: She doing alright?

RAY: Yeah.

She's not a not a natural sales person, really. Trying to get her to shift more padlocks.

JIM: Right.

RAY: Keep having to show her how to do the accounts, she can't remember.

JIM: Right.

RAY: She knows, she says she's not the right man for the job really... I mean, she doesn't mind filling in and–

JIM: Yeah.

RAY: Least it's January so it's quiet.

Pause.

You, um, you coming back then?

JIM: Don't know.

RAY: Elaine's been telling them you've got glandular fever.

RAY points at JIM's pile of door handles.

Help you with that?

JIM: If you want.

RAY sits down on the pile of doors and picks up a handle and a screwdriver.

RAY: Quite good really, cause glandular fever takes ages so–

JIM: Can do.

RAY: She wants me to ask you to come in tomorrow, quick visit.

JIM: No.

RAY: I told her it's all under control, I can handle it till you get back, and if she's there, for official decision making, bit like the queen, you know...

JIM: She's in charge.

RAY: Course, yeah.

She just said I should ask, cause of it being four weeks–
Says it's long enough, you know? Pass us another–

JIM passes RAY another door handle. RAY gestures towards the doors.

Why'd you um–

JIM: Oh, you know–

RAY: Meant to tell you – I worked it out.

JIM: What?

RAY: How to get into the units without the key. Trade secret. Worked it out myself.

JIM: Right.

RAY: S'alright I won't / tell her–

JIM: Don't need me at all then.

RAY: No, I – I mean it took ages it–

JIM: Keep thinking about her...

RAY: Elaine?

JIM: The woman. In the box.

RAY: Oh.

JIM: See her all the time. Red marks round her– (*Puts his hand to his neck.*). Stuffed in that box, all twisted up, big red mark round her neck, she looked, what was left of her, she looked pissed off. Her own dog lead I mean– You know? I– All that hair. She fucking stank and– the maggots and–

I keep thinking–

Beat. JIM looks at the floor.

RAY: She, um, she keeps crying. Elaine, she–

Pass us another.

JIM: All done now.

A long pause. ELAINE appears at the door to the garage.

There's these little fish, right...

RAY: Um–

JIM: I keep wondering if – Like maybe if I hadn't found her, maybe she wouldn't have been dead.

RAY: I don't really–

ELAINE and RAY exchange a look.

JIM: There's these little fish, little black ones and if you want to look at them you have to let them swim into your eye, like you have to put your head in the tank, in the water and–

JIM sees ELAINE out of the corner of his eye.

Hello, love.

So I put my head in the tank and let these fish swim into my eye and I could see them but then once I'd once I'd finished looking and took my head out it– It turned out one of the fish had swum behind my eye and got stuck and there's this optician trying to get it out with some kind of metal probe thing but when it finally flopped out this little black fish was bleeding and– Dead.

RAY: When was this?

ELAINE: It didn't happen.

RAY: Didn't know fish had blood.

ELAINE: It's a dream or…

JIM: Maybe in that second when I opened the box, maybe–
Like if I hadn't, maybe she'd have turned up at home a
few days later, she'd have– Maybe she– I don't know, just
wanted to disappear for a bit.

Maybe she'd have turned up at home, couple of days
later, she'd have just said 'I'm sorry. I needed some time
so I– I went to the seaside to think. And I'm sorry I didn't
call and I know you must have been really worried. But I
looked out at the sea and I knew I loved you so I've come
back. And I'm sorry it took a trip to Cleethorpes to get me
straightened out.'

RAY: Bit complicated / isn't it?

JIM: She went away to Cleethorpes to have a think, and if I
hadn't been there to find her in that box, she'd have come
back but the minute I saw her, that was it.

ELAINE: (*To RAY.*) Is he coming in?

JIM: No.

RAY: He says no.

ELAINE: We could say you didn't want to overdo it, maybe
the doctor said you had to be careful, take it slowly.

JIM: No.

RAY: Not sure if he's–

ELAINE: Cause you have to take it slowly with glandular
fever, so that's alright. Next week, maybe, just for a little
bit?

JIM: No.

ELAINE: Have a think about it at least.

JIM: I'm not going in.

> *Pause.*

ELAINE: Did / you–

RAY: I should–

ELAINE: OK.

> *RAY goes to leave. ELAINE catches his hand as he goes.*

Thanks, Ray.

> *ELAINE watches RAY go. Then she comes further into the garage and sits by JIM.*

Come on a bit, hasn't he?

> *She tries to touch JIM's hair, but he jerks away.*

Did you eat anything? I left your lunch in the fridge.

JIM: Not hungry.

ELAINE: OK. Well, you're– you're used to being so active, aren't you, probably burning less fuel... Pity, cause the freezer's stuffed with food we never ate at Christmas, what with the boys only being here a couple of days / instead of...

JIM: I can't stand the smell.

ELAINE: Just a turkey sandwich.

JIM: I've got the smell up my nose.

ELAINE: What smell?

JIM: B Sixteen.

> *ELAINE sighs.*

ELAINE: Right.

JIM: Just outside the door, and inside opening the box, my lungs got full of– Sticks like tar, it's stuck to the inside of my nose I can't get– Like one of the maggots crawled up and got stuck.

Beat.

ELAINE: Have you tried Vicks?

JIM: What?

ELAINE: I don't know, it might–

JIM: Not that kind of–

ELAINE: Just cause it's a strong smell, you know, it might– Or that Olbas Oil, same kind of thing, really.

JIM: Have you never– Got something stuck, a smell?

ELAINE: Not that I remember.

I mean, physically, it's not– I mean, is it?

JIM: I don't know *physically*.

ELAINE: Well it might help if you actually do something.

Beat.

But this is good.

JIM: What?

ELAINE: Talking about it. That's the thing, isn't it, talking about it?

JIM: Is it?

ELAINE: Well, that's the way it'll get better, isn't it?

JIM: I don't feel better.

ELAINE: You might have to talk about it more.

JIM shakes his head.

Might take some time.

JIM: I don't want to–

ELAINE: Jim.

JIM: I don't want to talk to Ray about it.

ELAINE: Just it was not talking about it buggered Christmas up, wasn't it?

Beat.

I'm here.

JIM looks away. ELAINE takes his hand. He pulls it away. ELAINE takes it again. They wrestle with their hands until ELAINE is only holding JIM's little finger. He lets her hang on, but turns the rest of himself away from her. He looks around the garage.

JIM: Never sat on the floor in here before. That thing where you see something from an angle you've never seen it before it all looks weird and…

ELAINE closes her eyes.

When I went in there– I felt– There was that smell and– It. It smelled a bit like. Sex. Like a room where you've been having sex. And I–

JIM looks at ELAINE.

You've got your eyes shut.

ELAINE opens her eyes.

ELAINE: No, just–

JIM: Why've you got your eyes shut?

ELAINE: I– Just listening.

JIM: I'm not saying any more.

ELAINE: I'm sorry. Please. Eyes open.

JIM: You think it's–

ELAINE: I just shut my eyes for a second, I'm sorry, I was listening. Please, I'll keep them open…

JIM: Right.

ELAINE: It smelled like–

JIM: Sex, yes.

ELAINE: I was letting you say it.

JIM: You didn't want to / say it.

ELAINE: I was letting you. It smelled like sex.

JIM: Yeah. And I got–

ELAINE: Did you?

JIM: Yeah.

JIM takes his hand away from ELAINE.

Sorry.

ELAINE: No– I don't–

JIM: And when I opened the box I was still– And I saw her– And I felt–

Pause.

I felt– I felt like– Elaine, I felt like I was the centre of the universe. I couldn't– I couldn't believe how how *important* I was. Less than a minute, standing there looking at her, hair all over her pissed-off face and I felt I felt I felt like a god.

ELAINE: God.

Silence.

JIM: I touched something, or– Or I was touched, I don't / know–

ELAINE: You touched her?

JIM: No I didn't bloody touch her, course I didn't–

Not saying any more.

Silence. JIM picks up the pill bottle and clicks the cap round and round.

ELAINE: Alright then. Can I say something?

I'm a bit– I'm a little bit sick of this. You let this mess up all of Christmas, our only time with the boys till what, a couple of days at Easter if we're lucky and you hardly said a word to anyone you'd barely look at them and I don't know if you noticed from in there but it was awful, Jim.

Cause bless them, they tried – taking you out to the pub and– and you just stared into your pint for an hour, no wonder they both went off straight after Boxing Day…

Will you stop clicking that, please?

JIM stops. He puts the bottle of pills on top of the pile of doors.

I mean I feel like. I feel like you're letting this get in the way when it really– It's a bit. I'm a bit– the doors and the talking rubbish about fish in your eyes and– I'm sorry it happened but I won't take responsibility and you shouldn't because we had nothing to do with it and we're not people that kill people and we're not–

I don't think you're trying. I can't believe how *unimportant* I–

Jim?

JIM: All feels a bit–

ELAINE: Bit what?

No answer.

A bit what?

JIM shakes his head. Beat.

I don't care about the business, if you don't want it anymore, fine, we'll sell it I don't care. But you'll have to do something else. You can't just stay at home taking the place apart with a screwdriver.

Jim, you've got to put the doors back. I won't be lonely, I can't do it.

JIM nods.

Will you?

JIM: What?

ELAINE: Put the doors back.

JIM: Bit tired from taking them all off, to be honest.

ELAINE: Right.

JIM: And I might sleep. If they're not there, if they're safe in here.

ELAINE: Oh god.

JIM: Cause I can't sleep, you see / and that's–

ELAINE: I know. But you've got your pills now so–

ELAINE puts her hands to her face.

JIM: Sorry.

ELAINE: Not sorry Jim, just do something.

ELAINE goes towards the door.

JIM: Put them back tomorrow.

ELAINE goes out. JIM remains on the floor and blows down each nostril in turn, as before. As he's doing so he catches sight of the bottle of pills on top of the doors.

Fade.

SCENE 5

Friday morning, late September, sunny with a heatwave starting tomorrow.

A hotel room, the same as in Scene 1.

Someone is lying in the bed, the sheets pulled up high. The figure is motionless.

AMY comes into the room with clean towels over her arm and a plastic carry-case of cleaning fluids.

She stops short when she sees the figure in the bed.

AMY: Oh god, sorry.

> *She goes to back out of the room, then stops again. She turns back slowly for a longer look at the figure in the bed.*
>
> Right.
>
> God not again.
>
> *She looks away. Bites her lip.*
>
> You're supposed to put the Do Not Disturb on. Then I wouldn't come barging in.
>
> *AMY takes a breath and goes over to the bed. She lifts the sheet and looks under it.*
>
> *Suddenly the figure moves, sits up, shouts, jumps out of bed. This is CHARLIE. He's just wearing boxer shorts.*
>
> *AMY gasps, backs away.*

CHARLIE: Who the fuck are / you?

AMY: Shit *fuck* sorry–

> *AMY backs away to the door.*
>
> Shit.

She leans against the door, her hand to her mouth, looking at CHARLIE. He's disarmingly attractive.

Sorry.

CHARLIE: What the fuck are you–

AMY: Sorry, house– housekeeping. You didn't put the– You didn't put the Do Not Disturb sign on I– And–

CHARLIE: What, you normally come and lift the sheets off people, did– Did you not see me? (*Looks at his watch.*) Shit–

AMY: What?

CHARLIE: Missed my alarm.

CHARLIE picks up his alarm clock.

Didn't set my alarm.

He looks at AMY. Sees she's still flattened against the door. Puts the clock down and takes a step towards her.

God, are you–

AMY: I thought you were dead.

CHARLIE: God, I– I mean crikey that'd be awful, wouldn't it?

AMY: You had the sheet pulled up over you, I–

CHARLIE: I I I always do, I–

AMY: I mean it looked–

CHARLIE: Why would you think I was dead?

AMY: Because–

CHARLIE: I mean, it must happen, but–

AMY: It happens quite a lot.

Beat.

Sorry. Come back later.

CHARLIE: It happens to you?

AMY: Sorry?

CHARLIE: It happens to you quite a lot?

AMY: Yes.

CHARLIE: Shit.

AMY: What?

CHARLIE: It, um, sorry, it suddenly occurs to me I'm just standing here in my boxers.

AMY looks away.

AMY: Sorry. I'll–

AMY puts her hand on the doorknob, to leave.

CHARLIE: No, hang on, wait. Don't–

AMY: Do the other rooms and come back I–

CHARLIE: No, just let me– I– I want to, you know, sort this out, I just think it'd be better if I had trousers on, if you could just–

CHARLIE goes to the wardrobe and opens it, takes out a pair of trousers.

If you could just hang on a second–

AMY: You can say at Reception–

CHARLIE: Sorry?

CHARLIE pulls the trousers on.

AMY: The manager's behind Reception this morning if you want to / complain.

CHARLIE: I don't. I don't want to complain.

AMY: Really?

CHARLIE: No. Yes, really.

I'm sorry I jumped out of bed shouting, I mean I was I was alarming, you were just as alarmed as I was / if not more...

AMY: Oh no, it's–

CHARLIE: I mean, if I'd managed to set my alarm for the right time – If I hadn't got totally sketched last night, completely knocked myself out–

AMY: Yeah.

CHARLIE: Just missing my alarm – that's what I'm pissed off about, not about you, you're–

CHARLIE looks at AMY.

God.

AMY: What?

CHARLIE: Nothing.

He holds his hand out to shake hers.

Charlie.

AMY: Amy.

Hi.

She shakes his hand.

CHARLIE: Pleasure to meet you.

AMY: Ooh–

CHARLIE: What?

AMY: Warm hands.

They smile at each other. She lets go of his hand.

Sorry.

I'll come back later.

CHARLIE: No, you can do it–

AMY: You'll not get any breakfast now, they stop at ten.

CHARLIE: Do you mind if I–

AMY: What?

CHARLIE: If I stick around while you–

AMY: Oh. Um, OK. It's not very interesting to watch, I–
OK.

You're here another night, yeah?

CHARLIE: Yeah.

AMY: OK.

CHARLIE: That makes a difference to–

AMY: If you're leaving I change the sheets.

CHARLIE: Course.

AMY smiles at him.

She takes a duster and polish from her cleaning kit and wipes the surfaces in the room. CHARLIE takes a shirt from the wardrobe and puts it on. He watches her out of the corner of his eye.

A slightly uncomfortable pause. AMY fills it.

AMY: Where'd you go?

CHARLIE: Sorry?

AMY: Last night, where'd you go, was it somewhere in town?

CHARLIE: Um, god it was– (*Thinking.*) Sorry, hungover,
um– Cocktail place, hammered metal lizards on the walls–

AMY: Iguana Bar.

CHARLIE: Yeah. Pretty shit, actually.

AMY: Don't go at the weekend, get your bum pinched five
times on the way to the loo.

175

CHARLIE: Well, I don't usually–

AMY: Town's a shithole, I'm afraid.

CHARLIE: Kind of place Dante'd draw circles round.

AMY: Who?

CHARLIE: Circles of hell, you know, the– the picture?

He draws circles in the air with his finger.

Beat.

So you find dead people quite often.

AMY: Not like Beachy Head or anything, not like it happens
every day, or– Not like it happens to anyone else, either,
just– My mum said I should maybe move to Beachy Head,
get a job at that hotel there, says they'd be used to people
like me–

CHARLIE: How many times?

AMY: Well. Two.

CHARLIE: Fuck.

AMY: So not that many really, just–

CHARLIE: No but *two*. That's got to be– I mean, god is that
usual for a hotel?

AMY: I don't think there's official figures–

CHARLIE: No, course. But– God, but I mean it's fascinating to
think, isn't it, all those hotels all over the country, all over
the world, all those people booking in to die, it's–

AMY: I don't like to–

CHARLIE: No. Sure, no. Kind of sick.

AMY: Well it's only two.

CHARLIE: Before and after, though, isn't it? The way you–

BREATHING CORPSES

CHARLIE breaks off, looks at AMY.

God–

AMY: What?

CHARLIE: Nothing, you're– Sorry, you're– Um, beautiful.

AMY: Oh, I'm–

CHARLIE: No, you are.

AMY: I'm in my stupid tabard, I–

CHARLIE: I'm sorry, I don't normally say things to– Sorry, do you / mind?

AMY: No, I– No.

Sorry, not supposed to argue when people say things… My mum says you should always just say thank you when someone says something.

Sorry I keep talking about my mum, do it when I'm nervous.

CHARLIE: Just thought I should say, so– Well, didn't think, really. Just said.

They smile at each other. He tries to hold her gaze but she looks away, moves to tidy around the tea tray.

AMY: You're not a tea drinker, then?

CHARLIE: Sorry?

AMY: You didn't touch the–

CHARLIE: Oh, no. Coffee, really.

AMY: Some coffee there.

CHARLIE: Can't drink instant.

AMY: Right.

CHARLIE: Most places I stay you can just call down for an espresso so–

AMY: Wow. Room service.

CHARLIE: Yeah.

AMY: Like five stars?

CHARLIE: Yeah.

AMY: Wow. I'd love to be in a five star hotel.

CHARLIE: Don't know if the pay's any better–

AMY: Stay in one.

CHARLIE: Right. You should.

AMY: Can't afford it.

CHARLIE: Someone should take you.

I'll take you.

AMY: You're joking.

CHARLIE: Up to you.

AMY: No, you're joking.

CHARLIE: I don't do jokes.

Again, AMY breaks his gaze, goes back to dusting.

AMY: Shame. Girls like a sense of humour.

CHARLIE: Thing is the um, the only kind of jokes I can ever remember are a bit, um a bit sick.

AMY: Like what?

CHARLIE: Um, no it's a bit sick.

AMY: Go on.

CHARLIE: No, I–

AMY: OK, I'll finish up later, then, leave you in / peace.

She goes to leave.

CHARLIE: What d'you get if you put a baby in a blender?

AMY: What?

CHARLIE: What d'you get if you put a baby in a blender?

AMY: What?

CHARLIE: A stiffy.

Beat.

AMY: That is a bit sick.

CHARLIE: Yeah. Sorry.

AMY stifles a giggle.

AMY: Just do the bathroom.

AMY takes the towels, plus a bottle of cleaning spray and a cloth into the bathroom. CHARLIE sits on the bed.

He stands and goes towards his suitcase and stretches his hand out towards it, then stops.

Looks towards the bathroom. Moves away from the suitcase, his hand on the back of his neck.

A moment, then he goes back to the suitcase rapidly and takes out a shallow, rectangular black box. He puts it down on the bedside table, touches the top of the box then moves away again.

Looks towards the bathroom.

CHARLIE: What was it like, finding those people?

AMY comes to the bathroom door.

AMY: Pardon?

CHARLIE: Was it terrible, when you found those people, the dead ones?

AMY: Oh right.

AMY goes back into the bathroom.

It was– It kind of wasn't, it was kind of normal. D'you think that's awful?

CHARLIE: No.

AMY comes back to the bathroom door.

AMY: Pardon?

CHARLIE: I said no. It's not awful. If that's how you felt.

AMY: I felt old, mostly.

AMY goes back into the bathroom and carries on cleaning.

Just get on with it, don't you?

CHARLIE sits down on the edge of the bed with the box on his lap. He opens it and takes out a Japanese carving knife with an ornate horn and ebony handle. He handles it with some confidence, but you can tell it's incredibly sharp.

I mean, yeah, the first one was really hard, I'd never seen a dead person before and she was really– really young. Like my age.

CHARLIE: Christ.

CHARLIE looks towards the bathroom door, the knife in his hand.

AMY: Right mess, as well. Sick all over the sheets and blood and stuff...

Actually the second one was worse, he was older, he was a dad and it wasn't that long after the first one so I hadn't really got over that yet and now it's like, like a pattern...

CHARLIE puts the knife back in the box, puts it quietly back on the dressing table.

Manager thinks I'm the angel of death or something, won't let me work on Bank Holidays now. Quite a relief when you sat up and swore at me, really.

AMY comes out of the bathroom.

All done.

She sees the black box on the dressing table.

What's that?

CHARLIE stands up.

CHARLIE: It's– I uh– It's a product I'm delivering to a client today.

AMY: A product?

CHARLIE: I um, I supply kitchen equipment.

AMY: Pots and pans.

CHARLIE: Special, hand made stuff.

AMY: Can I see?

CHARLIE: I um. Yeah.

CHARLIE holds the box open towards AMY.

AMY: It's a knife.

CHARLIE: Yeah.

AMY: A kitchen knife?

CHARLIE: Yes.

AMY: Doesn't look like a kitchen knife.

CHARLIE: It's for a special kind of Japanese cuisine. More about worship than practicality, really.

AMY: Can I hold it?

CHARLIE: It's fucking sharp.

AMY: OK.

AMY takes out the knife and holds it. CHARLIE has to sit down.

CHARLIE: Beautiful, yeah?

LAURA WADE

AMY: Pattern on it. Looks like wood, not metal.

CHARLIE: Multi-layered steel. Hand-forged. Breath–
Breathtakingly sharp.

CHARLIE looks up, sees AMY looking at him intently.

What?

AMY: You're all lit up, your eyes are shining.

CHARLIE: Oh. Right, I–

AMY: It's nice.

They smile at each other. AMY puts the knife back in the box.

Do the bed now–

CHARLIE: Right.

AMY: Last thing.

CHARLIE moves awkwardly from the bed to the stool by the dressing table. AMY goes to the bed and starts to make it.

CHARLIE takes his shoes and socks and starts to put them on, watching AMY.

There isn't really anything to say. He keeps watching her after he's done his shoes and socks. She knows he's watching and occasionally smiles – it's nice to have someone there.

CHARLIE: OK.

AMY: What?

CHARLIE: Should get some breakfast.

AMY: You're going?

CHARLIE: Get something to eat. Suddenly hungry.

AMY: I could get chef to do you a bacon sarnie. Egg on toast.

CHARLIE picks up his wallet and keys.

CHARLIE: Might pop into town.

AMY: OK. Good luck.

CHARLIE goes to leave.

CHARLIE: Meet me later.

AMY: I–

CHARLIE: Get a drink or something.

AMY: I can't, I've got to wait on in the restaurant, then I'm on
    bar all evening, we're a bit short-staffed–

CHARLIE: What time d'you finish?

AMY: Midnight.

CHARLIE: A drink at midnight, then. Celebration drink.

AMY: I don't–

CHARLIE: Maybe we've broken the pattern, you know
    – maybe you'll never find another one–

AMY: Oh don't–

CHARLIE: What?

AMY: Tempting fate.

CHARLIE: Bugger fate, you know? I'd take you somewhere
    nice.

AMY: No, I– I'll be tired, I should go home. But thanks.

CHARLIE: Tomorrow, then?

AMY: On till midnight again.

CHARLIE: What time d'you start?

AMY: Breakfast. Eight o'clock.

CHARLIE: Long day.

AMY: I'm sorry, just– You're a guest. Not allowed. Already
    sailing close to the–

CHARLIE: What about early – tomorrow morning, early? No-one around then.

AMY: I can't–

CHARLIE: Coffee or a walk in the park or something? Or– Or I don't know. Just I've got to head off tomorrow.

You know, I wake up this morning and it turns out I'm not dead, and that's– I mean, isn't it? That's remarkable, surely. And if I wake up tomorrow not dead I'd like to see you before I leave. Cause who knows – you know, tomorrow I might crash the Boxster, wrap it round a lamp post. Or a pedestrian. And I like you a lot.

AMY: A Boxster.

CHARLIE: Porsche.

AMY: I know.

CHARLIE: You'd look great in it. See it if you look out.

AMY goes to the curtains and looks at the car park.

The silver one. Convertible.

What d'you think? Meet me at seven tomorrow, a drive if you like, or a walk in the park, don't have to decide now… It's going to be a gorgeous day – hottest September on record, they're saying. You should get out in it.

AMY: OK.

CHARLIE: Yes?

AMY: Yeah.

CHARLIE comes close to AMY, looks into her eyes.

CHARLIE: You're luminous.

AMY frowns.

You glow.

CHARLIE kisses his thumb and places it on AMY's forehead.

Tomorrow.

AMY nods. CHARLIE leaves.

AMY finishes making the bed. She catches sight of the knife box on the bedside table, and looks to the door to check CHARLIE isn't coming back. Then, she opens the box and looks at the knife. She touches it with her fingertips, but doesn't take it out of the box.

AMY closes the box and looks around her. She starts to dust again, smiling, distracted, looking at the door CHARLIE went through, not noticing she's cleaned the surfaces already. After a few seconds she gives in and decides to enjoy the moment.

She sits down on the edge of the bed and laughs to herself, quietly, her hand to her mouth.

The end.

OTHER HANDS

For Rod

My sincerest thanks to the following for their help with the development of *Other Hands*:
Tamara Harvey, Michael Shaw, Jack Thorne, Charlotte Mann, Jamie Carmichael, Gabriel Winn, Tina and Stuart Wade, Bijan Sheibani, Nina Steiger, Jon Lloyd and all at Soho Theatre.

Plus anyone else who had a hand in it. Thank you.

LW, February 2006

Characters

STEVE, 31

LYDIA, 34

HAYLEY, 30

GREG, 45

Other Hands was first performed at Soho Theatre on 15 February 2006, with the following cast:

GREG, Michael Gould
STEVE, Richard Harrington
HAYLEY, Anna Maxwell Martin
LYDIA, Katherine Parkinson

Director Bijan Sheibani
Designer Paul Burgess
Lighting Designer Guy Kornetskzi
Sound Designer Emma Laxton

SCENE 1

LYDIA's studio flat. Late morning.

LYDIA is standing in front of the computer, looking at STEVE. He stands by the door, a motorbike helmet in his hand. The air fizzes.

LYDIA: You've got an hour.

STEVE: Um

LYDIA: What?

STEVE: It's. I can't predict how long it's

LYDIA: How long

STEVE: I mean, it can take longer

LYDIA: Longer than an hour?

STEVE: Well, it. I don't always know till I. Start. How long I'm going to be doing it for is all

LYDIA: Right. Well / I

STEVE: Sometimes it's just thirty seconds or so sometimes and sometimes it's I do try and keep it as quick as possible but

LYDIA: OK

STEVE: But it can take longer and I can't really tell until I, you know, get down to it

LYDIA: Get down to it

STEVE: Have a go

LYDIA: You don't think with your, your experience you should be able to predict

Because I did tell you quite clearly what I wanted on the phone

193

STEVE: There's lots of

LYDIA: And you are a *professional* so

STEVE: I mean it just isn't possible to

    Beat.

LYDIA: I can only afford an hour.

STEVE: Right.

LYDIA: Sorry.

STEVE: No

LYDIA: I should have said on the phone

STEVE: OK

LYDIA: So

STEVE: Well let's give it an hour and see how we go.

LYDIA: OK.

    STEVE puts his helmet down and moves towards the PC.

STEVE: It's the modem, you said

LYDIA: God, I don't know, I mean

    God knows what's going on in there just won't connect to the internet

STEVE: Since

LYDIA: Monday

STEVE: OK well let's

LYDIA: I might not be using the right words, the terminology

    LYDIA is still standing in front of the PC, barring STEVE's way.

STEVE: Can I

LYDIA: Um

STEVE: Have a look?

LYDIA: Um, yeah

LYDIA starts to move away, then darts back to stand between STEVE and the computer.

Sorry

STEVE: What?

LYDIA: Sorry I just

Thing is I can't let you *start*, you see, because

If you start and then we get to the end of the hour and it isn't fixed, and you. I'm not questioning you know, but. If it isn't fixed and you go away, or it's worse because I don't know, you've run some kind of programme on it and now it's worse it's made all sorts of crawlies come out of the. I mean I'm not saying you would, you know, but

I mean then I'm

Then I'm *really* stuck

STEVE: Yeah

LYDIA: I really need it, I

STEVE: Yeah. Yeah

LYDIA: And you, you did say that. You know, sometimes, doesn't it, it takes more than an hour you said and I can't afford it because

And you can't tell, can you, with people, sometimes it's an hour and five minutes and you get charged for the second hour, for breaking into it but I really

I mean, when I say I can't afford it it's not that I think it *shouldn't* take longer than an hour, like I'm opposed to the idea of paying for this this service that you do, which I actually think is a great idea and you know it's a godsend for people like me so it's not that I don't agree with the idea of paying more than forty pounds it's just that

I mean I just don't have it, I really can't.

I'm sorry

STEVE: No, I

LYDIA: I should have said before

STEVE: No

LYDIA: 'Stead of making you come all the way over here from

STEVE: Fulham

LYDIA: Fulham. Oh, not too far

STEVE: Not too far, no

LYDIA: Quite direct on a bike I should thi

STEVE: I, um

LYDIA: I'm sorry. I really am.

Beat.

STEVE: I could

LYDIA: Yes?

STEVE: You could just pay me for the hour and I'll. I'll stay till it's done.

LYDIA exhales. Smiles.

LYDIA: Yes. Yeah. Thank you

She moves away from the PC.

You see that's. That's kind. That's *kind*

Thank you.

STEVE: Sure.

STEVE sits down at the PC. He flexes his fingers.

LYDIA: So what if it's less than an hour?

STEVE: What?

LYDIA: Joke. Sorry, joke. Just, joke.

STEVE smiles. LYDIA sits down on the bed.

STEVE: You don't have to stay with me if you

LYDIA: It's a studio

STEVE: Right, sorry

LYDIA: Unless you'd like a cup of tea, or

STEVE: No thanks

LYDIA: Or water or

I think I've got some squash, some kind of weird combination like strawberry and apricot or

STEVE: I'm OK.

LYDIA: Don't know why I bought it really, sounds disgusting. Not very grown-up, is it, squash?

STEVE moves the mouse, then frowns.

STEVE: Does it always crash like this?

LYDIA: Oh. Yeah, always. All the time. Hit 'save' every five seconds now.

STEVE: You work from home, do you?

LYDIA: No, I. No.

Pause. STEVE reboots the PC. LYDIA watches him.

God, you must. You must really see some stuff

Things people have on their machines

STEVE: Don't really look

LYDIA: No?

STEVE: Not really interested

LYDIA: No

Beat.

No? You must be a little bit?

STEVE: Maybe a / bit

LYDIA: A little bit. Curious.

STEVE: Most people there's not

LYDIA: Well you won't find any porn on there

LYDIA laughs and looks away.

STEVE: What you do with your personal

LYDIA: My *personal*

STEVE: It's none of my business

LYDIA: I don't have anything *personal* on

STEVE: I'm just here to fix it

Beat.

LYDIA: There's someone I email, OK?

And if. If I can't email, then

And I haven't been able to email for days so I feel a bit

STEVE: OK

LYDIA: But I wouldn't

I wouldn't want you to read any of the emails, so

STEVE: I won't

LYDIA: I haven't met him

I

It's ridiculous really, but

STEVE: I won't

LYDIA: Read them, no

STEVE peers at the screen.

STEVE: Shit

LYDIA: What? What?

STEVE: I'm going to be here a while.

Fade.

SCENE 2

GREG's office. Late afternoon.

GREG and HAYLEY are drinking coffee from vending-machine cups.
GREG is emptying sachets of sugar into his.

HAYLEY: You don't seem convinced.

GREG: I'm not.

HAYLEY: I'm afraid the board are.

GREG: Seduced, aren't they?

 Flashy logos, big words. Sugar?

HAYLEY: No thank you

 He offers her a sachet.

GREG: Sweetener?

HAYLEY: No

GREG: Sweet enough

HAYLEY: I like it bitter

 We're going to have to work together

GREG: Oh I know

HAYLEY: And an atmosphere, we've found, an atmosphere of
 hostility can only serve to make the process more

GREG: Painful

HAYLEY: Less comfortable for your department, the staff. If
 they see that you're

GREG: Hostile

HAYLEY: Uncomfortable

Because what we're doing really isn't it's not a revolution it's just

Incremental change that will rationalise

GREG: Feels like a revolution

HAYLEY: Because it's new and it's not familiar

If we work together, we can turn it round.

GREG takes a sip of his coffee and pulls a face.

GREG: Christ. Get them to put in a new coffee machine I've never managed to get that changed

HAYLEY: This really isn't a reflection on your

When you've been in something so long, it's hard to step back and have a look, isn't it, see the big picture. Impossible for anyone to know how to fix something that

GREG: They all think they're going to lose their jobs, you know. People coming to me every five minutes, 'Are there going to be job losses?'

HAYLEY: There may be opportunities to *upskill* the labour force and

GREG: They feel watched, you know, what can I say to that? Threatened

HAYLEY: But if for example we were to incentivise

GREG: Incentivise like I have to do such and such hit such and such a target if I want to keep my

HAYLEY: Not you personally. Your position's safe, you're fine

GREG: Yours as well, I presume, what've you got riding on this?

HAYLEY: I don't think that's

GREG: Be sad if you lost that snazzy little motor, what is it, little sporty thing?

HAYLEY: TVR

GREG: Good er, handling?

HAYLEY: It roars I like it.

GREG: Flashy

HAYLEY: What do you drive?

GREG: I sometimes

I sometimes look at, you know, someone like you and I think what do you know, really? What do you know about any of this, how young you are, you've never

HAYLEY: It isn't a case of

GREG: I started out stacking shelves, you know.

HAYLEY: Assistant Manager, wasn't it?

GREG looks at her.

HR file

GREG: It was a small branch. They gave you my file?

HAYLEY: I'm doing a Human Performance Review, I have to understand the humans involved

GREG: And I'm not under threat?

HAYLEY: No

The company's always had a strong policy of rewarding loyalty, long-term service, always has. But sometimes that isn't all / you

GREG: Are you saying

HAYLEY: It's possible we have the specialist knowledge

GREG: I don't?

HAYLEY: And the time, we have time, I mean with all the things you have to do do you have time to do this kind of project?

GREG: I'd cost less

HAYLEY: With all the, just the day to day, keeping an eye on the day to day, whereas we have the time and the objectivity and the expertise to

GREG's mobile rings.

D'you want to

GREG: No, no, it's

HAYLEY: I don't mind

GREG looks at the phone.

GREG: Bloody hell

He picks it up.

Yes love. Yes, I'm in a. Can't you handle it, I'm in a

What's wrong with him?

His what? What kind of. Do they look

Is that him in the. Put him on the phone. Because I might be able to

Well if you had to ring me at work. Will you just put him on the phone, so I can see what's. Thank you.

GREG looks at HAYLEY.

HAYLEY: Everything alright?

GREG: My son's being

Jonathan? Mum says you won't do your homework.

What's wrong with your hands? What kind of

Where? What your wrist, or fingers or

Have you taken. OK. Well it should, half an hour it should kick in

You know what this is, don't you? It's that bloody X-Box, that's what it is, isn't it? How much homework have you

OK, give it half an hour for the Nurofen to kick in, OK, then get on with it, I'll be home at what, half seven, I want to see your Maths finished and on the kitchen table, yes?

Or you won't be going out with your mates for the rest of the month, that's what. OK? Put your mother ba

Jonathan has hung up. GREG puts the phone down. Looks at it. Presses a button to switch it off.

(*To HAYLEY.*) Don't have kids.

HAYLEY: I might one day

GREG: Stay as you are

Says his fingers hurt so he can't do his homework. Lazy sod.

Boy doesn't seem to have any idea what he wants to do with his life

HAYLEY: How old?

GREG: Fifteen

HAYLEY: Well, *fifteen*

Did you know at fifteen?

GREG: Wasn't so much choice back then

Did you know?

HAYLEY: Didn't know what a management consultant was when I was fifteen

GREG: I'm still not sure

HAYLEY: You've done well for yourself, even if it's not what you thought / you'd

GREG: I mean I'm still not sure what a management consultant is

Beat.

I'm baiting you, being hostile

HAYLEY: Noted

GREG: You can put it in your report

HAYLEY: I'm sorry this is difficult for you. The company's been very slow to get consultants involved, you've got peers in other companies that've been working with people like me for years they're quite used to it, don't see us as a threat at all

GREG: So we're backward

HAYLEY: No

There *is* room for more *forward-thinking*

GREG looks at her.

So

OK

We'll be on site from Monday, have a look at processes as they stand, progress it from there. Um. There'll be a couple of consultants and a team of analysts working into me and they'll / be

GREG: 'Working into'?

HAYLEY: Um

GREG: (*He mimes a wriggling worm with his finger.*) 'Working *into* me'

HAYLEY: Working *for* me, then

GREG: Sounds a bit

Rude

HAYLEY: Well, they'll be here, my team, so if you could accommodate them that / would be

GREG: Won't you be here?

HAYLEY: I'll be in and out, I'll be around

Perhaps if you and I sit down together again in a week or so, touch base then, then we'll be in a position to actually leverage

GREG: 'Leverage', isn't it?

HAYLEY: Sorry?

GREG: Don't we pronounce it 'leverage' in this country?

HAYLEY: I

GREG: Bet you say 'oriented', not 'orientated' as well, don't you?

HAYLEY takes her Palm Pilot out of the laptop bag at her feet.

HAYLEY: It's an American consultancy, there's a culture

GREG: Leverage

HAYLEY: Shall we look at schedules?

GREG: 'Schedules'

HAYLEY: How's next / Wednesday?

GREG: I don't do my diary, my secretary

HAYLEY: Or Thursday morning? Friday afternoon?

HAYLEY slides the Palm Pilot out of its case with a little effort. GREG looks at the case and picks it up.

GREG: Broken.

HAYLEY: Yes, I.

You know, how you get. Used to things

GREG: What d'you mean?

HAYLEY: You know, something gets broken and I

I never have time to you know, fix it properly so it gets sellotaped and then you kind of modify your behaviour and you get used to the sellotape and

You get used to it being broken, you adapt.

GREG looks at her.

Not with a project, with personal

GREG: You let your guard down for a second then

HAYLEY: It won't happen again.

GREG: I rather liked it.

HAYLEY looks at her coffee. GREG leans back in his chair.

Fade.

SCENE 3

Kitchen/Living area of HAYLEY and STEVE's flat. Evening.

STEVE is on the Playstation. HAYLEY is unpacking groceries from a plastic bag on the counter.

HAYLEY: Huh

STEVE: What?

HAYLEY: Bread-bin

STEVE: On the counter

HAYLEY: I know, but

We never put the bread in it, do we, we always put the bread next to it. Why do we do that?

STEVE: I'unno

HAYLEY: I mean, that's

She starts to put the new bread inside the bread-bin.

I'm putting it inside, OK?

No answer.

Steve, the bread's in the bread-bin, OK?

Looking inside the bread-bin.

Last year's green bagel is no longer in the bread-bin, it's in the bin.

She puts the old bagel in the bin, then looks in the bread-bin again.

This is disgusting. There's crumbs in here from when we moved in. Was it my mother got us this or yours?

No answer. She wipes inside the bread-bin with a cloth.

You know, you could unplug yourself and talk to me. Ask me how my day was

STEVE: How was your day?

HAYLEY: Doesn't count

STEVE: What?

HAYLEY: You have to have taken your hands off the controls and turned the screen off

STEVE: I'm nearly

HAYLEY: And be facing me

HAYLEY boils the kettle and prepares a mug for tea.

STEVE: Just finish this level

HAYLEY: You could ask me how my big meeting was

STEVE: How was your meeting?

HAYLEY: He was a wanker. Greg the wanker

STEVE: Everyone you work for's a wanker.

HAYLEY: You know the weirdest thing happened to me on the way home tonight. The weirdest thing. Coming back from work and I was driving, the same way I always drive, like every day and

I got to a junction, lots of little roads going off it and. God, I suddenly I couldn't remember which way I was going, which way was home. The same way I go every day, like on autopilot but suddenly

Like the light was different or. Or I was different. I don't know

STEVE: Shit

HAYLEY: What?

STEVE: Died

HAYLEY opens the fridge.

HAYLEY: Oh, *Steve*

STEVE: What?

HAYLEY: There's no fucking milk. Did you finish the milk?

STEVE: Sorry

HAYLEY: You couldn't have

STEVE: You just went to the supermarket

HAYLEY: There was loads this morning

STEVE: I drank some

HAYLEY: You could have called me I mean

STEVE: Hayley, it's

You know, calm down

HAYLEY: Well when did when did we get so bloody inefficient?

STEVE: Over-reaction

HAYLEY: I don't think it is

Beat.

Sorry, I'm tired

Got to go to this party.

STEVE: Fuck, is that tonight?

HAYLEY: I've got to socialise with these people it's. You know, if I'm trying to make partner next year. It's important

STEVE: OK, so we're going

HAYLEY: I am. You you said you didn't want to

STEVE: No, I'll come

HAYLEY: OK.

HAYLEY gets the ironing board and the iron out of a cupboard and sets them up. She goes out of the room and returns a moment later with a pair of trousers and a top. She irons the trousers during the following.

What did you do today?

STEVE: I did a job

HAYLEY: Did you?

STEVE: Woman in Putney. Viruses. Rebuilt it from scratch

HAYLEY: God, how long did that

STEVE: 'Bout six hours

HAYLEY: God, so that's (*Adding it up.*) two hundred and / forty

STEVE: Forty

HAYLEY: Yes, two hundred and forty

STEVE: Forty. I got forty pounds.

HAYLEY: For six hours?

STEVE: She. She only had forty pounds so we made a deal

HAYLEY: Steve, your first job in a week and you made a

STEVE: She wanted to sort it out before I started and I didn't know if it was going to take six hours or six minutes, so

And I was

HAYLEY: What?

STEVE: She really needed it

HAYLEY: What for work?

STEVE: No, I don't know for. Some bloke she was emailing

HAYLEY: What, a boyfriend?

STEVE: She hadn't met him

HAYLEY: You made a deal so she could play the fucking personals?

STEVE: She was really upset

HAYLEY fiddles with the controls on the iron, frowning, half watching STEVE.

HAYLEY: D'you know how this fucking

No of course you don't

HAYLEY pours water into the iron.

Was she pretty?

STEVE: Lonely, I think

HAYLEY: Everyone's lonely

STEVE looks back to his game, picks up the handset.

Forty pounds isn't

For a week

You'd get more on the dole. You'd get more on the fucking game, Steve, even with your complete lack of

There's a vacancy at work. IT Support Manager

Thirty grand starting salary

STEVE: No

HAYLEY: We'd see more of each other

STEVE: I left, we had a cake. Said 'fuck it' on the top

HAYLEY: 'Fuck I.T.', wasn't it?

Six hours for forty pounds. Hope she gave you a cup of tea

STEVE puts the handset down and flexes his fingers.

Did you call the doctor?

STEVE: Just stiff from doing that job

HAYLEY: Playstation

STEVE: No, it's not

HAYLEY: It's the only repeated action you do. Just go to the doctor, get it sorted.

You know you don't get any sympathy until you get it looked at

HAYLEY finishes ironing the trousers and changes into them. STEVE goes to the fridge.

If you're coming we've got to go

STEVE: Yeah

STEVE takes a can of Fanta out of the fridge. He opens it, drinks, then looks at HAYLEY, who is frowning.

Alright

STEVE takes a glass from the cupboard and pours some Fanta into it. He watches the froth go down, intently. Sees HAYLEY watching him again.

What?

HAYLEY: I still don't know how you work. All this time. How your brain works.

STEVE: Bit of a fucking mystery yourself.

HAYLEY: Kiss me.

STEVE makes a kissing sound with his lips. He goes back to sit at the Playstation. HAYLEY prepares to iron her top, stretching it out on the ironing board to smooth out creases. STEVE flexes his fingers. HAYLEY sees this.

You don't have to come if it's hurting.

HAYLEY picks up the iron and knocks the plastic water jug to the floor.

Dammit

She picks it up from the floor, then irons the top. It's quite a complicated garment.

STEVE: You don't want me to come

HAYLEY: Put your shoes on

STEVE: You asked me to come

HAYLEY: Yeah, but

STEVE: You asked me last week

HAYLEY: You said you didn't want to

STEVE: I said I didn't want to, it doesn't mean I'm not going

HAYLEY: Well you should have made it clear 'cause I've got used to the idea of you not coming now

And I've arranged to meet Nick off the Tube.

STEVE: He won't mind

HAYLEY: I would

STEVE: Yeah but you're

HAYLEY: What?

STEVE: I dunno

HAYLEY: Well if you're coming put your shoes on

You're wearing that, yeah?

STEVE: What would you like me to wear?

HAYLEY: Just. That's fine, what you've got on

STEVE: I could wear the black / one

HAYLEY: It's fine it's just a house party

STEVE: Where are my

HAYLEY: There

STEVE: Where?

HAYLEY: By the sofa

STEVE: No, not the

HAYLEY: You're not going in your trainers, god

STEVE: You said it was just a house / party

HAYLEY: Please, for me, just wear your nice shoes

STEVE picks up the shoes and sits down on the sofa. He puts them on carefully.

And don't tell any jokes

STEVE: Which one's Nick?

HAYLEY: Nick from work Nick

STEVE looks at HAYLEY.

You've met him

STEVE: All look the same

HAYLEY: You talked about Doom

STEVE: OK

HAYLEY: Then you told him the stupid 'how we met' story

STEVE: He probably asked

HAYLEY: Yeah no, I remember

About half way through I looked at us, like from a few steps away and I realised we were being really irritating. This routine telling it the exact same way and it's really not the greatest story is it not really and I fucking hate that

STEVE: What?

HAYLEY: With couples when you talk to them or discussing something with them and you can tell they've had the same conversation before they're just doing it again, we've started doing that

STEVE: We can talk to people separately.

Pause. HAYLEY puts her top on.

HAYLEY: You know I think I might stop

I might just *stop talking* 'cause everything I say feels like I've said it before every fucking thing sounds like I've rehearsed it I just have to open my mouth and I piss myself off

STEVE: You shouldn't

HAYLEY: What?

STEVE: Everyone gets

HAYLEY: Do they? I'm even less special than I thought

You ready?

She sees STEVE having trouble with the laces on his shoes.

Steve, you can't even do your laces, you've got to go to the doctor. 'Cause don't think I'll be here when it gets to not being able to wipe your own arse.

STEVE: It's fine

HAYLEY kneels down and starts to tie STEVE's shoe-laces.

HAYLEY: Let me / do it

STEVE: You don't have to

HAYLEY: I'm not being sympathetic I'm trying not to be late we've got to go

STEVE: My trainers are Velcro so

HAYLEY: Yep

HAYLEY finishes tying the laces.

OK. Handbag

HAYLEY picks up her bag and coat.

Come on

They go out into the hallway. A moment.

HAYLEY comes back in.

Wait. Wait.

She unplugs the iron and winds the cord up neatly and tucks it into the handle.

Two seconds.

She puts the iron and the board away, then looks around at the room. She is still for a moment.

Steve?

STEVE: (*Off.*) Yeah?

HAYLEY: I want to sleep with someone else.

Pause. STEVE comes back and stands in the doorway.

STEVE: Who?

HAYLEY: I don't know yet.

Fade.

SCENE 4

LYDIA's studio flat. A week later. Late afternoon.

STEVE and LYDIA face each other, as at the start of Scene 1.

LYDIA: Nice to see you

STEVE: I can't stay today

　　You know, if it takes

　　If it takes longer than however long you

LYDIA: No, I can afford you today. And it's nice to see you

　　I've said that.

　　LYDIA smiles.

STEVE: So, um

LYDIA: It's the printer

STEVE: Oh

LYDIA: It won't. Print

STEVE: Right

LYDIA: Obvious, really, I mean that's all I need it to do

　　I've got to get. Got to start applying for a job and there'll
　　be CVs and letters and. So I'll need it

STEVE: Thing is I don't

　　Don't really do printers

LYDIA: Oh

STEVE: Mostly there's enough in the handbook to sort it out if
　　there's something not working

LYDIA: I just assumed it's all

STEVE: And if the handbook doesn't help then usually you just replace it, get a new one

LYDIA: Oh god

STEVE: 'Cause they're not that expensive so there's usually no point fixing them, you just get a new one

LYDIA: I've only just worked out how this one works

When it's working

STEVE: See most of them these days they've got a built-in obsolescence, they're designed to only last a few years so

Have you looked at the

LYDIA: Handbook

STEVE: Yes

LYDIA: Think I've lost it

STEVE: Have you, sorry if this is obvious, have you done stuff like checked the paper tray, checked it's got ink, that sort of

LYDIA: It tells me, on the little display when it's, when it needs paper, or. Gives the illusion of being user-friendly

I'm sorry, I didn't know you didn't do

STEVE: What's it say now?

LYDIA looks at the display on the printer.

LYDIA: Machine Error 41

STEVE frowns.

I know, I mean, what does that mean, you know?

STEVE: Probably says in the

LYDIA: Handbook, yeah

Beat. They look at each other.

STEVE: RTFM

LYDIA: Sorry?

STEVE: Geek-speak. Read The Fucking Manual.

LYDIA smiles.

Have you looked online?

LYDIA: Didn't think of that

STEVE: Give it a try

LYDIA: I don't suppose, since you're here, you couldn't

I know it's not your remit really but you'll still know more about it than I do and

STEVE: OK

LYDIA pulls the computer chair out for STEVE to sit on.

LYDIA: Thank you

STEVE goes to sit down at the computer.

STEVE: But this is working, yeah?

LYDIA: Oh yes. Yes. No problems at all, thank you

Haven't actually used it that much this week

STEVE: I thought it was really

LYDIA: Yeah. Well. We were emailing every day, now we're not so

Now we're not at all.

We were arranging to meet each other, then he just
stopped

Beat. LYDIA goes to the kitchen.

You know, I wasn't lying last week when I said I couldn't
pay more it's just I

LYDIA returns with two glasses of squash.

got a new credit card.

STEVE: No, I didn't mean to

LYDIA puts one of the glasses down next to STEVE.

Thanks.

It's just my girlfriend's on my back about undercharging
people so

LYDIA: Course. Course she is.

LYDIA smiles weakly. STEVE looks at the squash.

STEVE: You don't um, happen to have a straw at all

LYDIA: A straw?

STEVE: Drinking straw

LYDIA: Oh. Yeah, think so

LYDIA goes to the kitchen to look.

You know, when I said it was nice to see you I meant, I
didn't mean

I was just I was so glad you helped me, felt like I was going
mad.

STEVE: Yeah

LYDIA: Surrounded by all this stuff and I don't know how any of it works, the computer and the CD player, can't even work out how to change the ring tone on my phone so it pisses me off every time it rings, not that it rings very often, all these microchips all these passwords and PIN codes

LYDIA comes back with a straw. Hands it to STEVE.

I mean I just don't feel *equipped*

STEVE: Yeah

STEVE puts the straw in his squash.

LYDIA: Like at school in Physics they taught us how to wire a plug, but that's about as far as I

STEVE bends down to drink his squash through the straw. LYDIA watches him, distracted for a second.

Um

STEVE goes back to looking at the screen.

And things come with fitted plugs now anyway, so.

STEVE: Here we go, there's some stuff on here…

LYDIA goes to stand beside him.

LYDIA: And like, when I get another job. If

I've only been out of work four months but they've probably changed the technology since then so I've got another photocopier to make friends with, work out what the fax means when it beeps at me

STEVE: Yeah.

STEVE glances at LYDIA, then back at the screen.

LYDIA: I had a good job

She looks at her hands.

STEVE: What was it?

LYDIA: Office Manager

STEVE laughs.

LYDIA laughs.

I know. Brilliant, isn't it?

LYDIA looks out of the window, stops laughing.

I loved it, actually

Then I took my first two-week holiday since I'd started there and some consultants came in, shook things up

By the time I came back they'd realised they didn't need an Office Manager, hadn't missed me at all. Turned out they could um, manage.

What's she like, your girlfriend?

STEVE: Why?

LYDIA: Curious

STEVE: She's. Efficient. Always pre-heats the oven.

She likes air-fresheners, every room in our house smells different. Never room to plug anything in, all these little plastic gel things

They smile at each other. STEVE looks back at the screen.

It's fatal

LYDIA: What?

STEVE: Error 41. You'd have to replace the

How long have you had it?

LYDIA: Three years?

STEVE: Thing is after that long it's out of warranty, anyway, so to replace the print-head that's going to cost you like

Well you might as well get a new one

LYDIA nods.

Sorry.

LYDIA: Get one on the credit card, then

STEVE: Tottenham Court Road

LYDIA: Right

STEVE: Lots of places along there, see if you can get a two-year warranty on it.

LYDIA: D'you think they'll see me coming? Red light on the door that flashes when a clueless bit of fluff walks in?

STEVE: You're not clueless, most people don't

LYDIA: Yeah, I guess.

STEVE stands.

So

STEVE: I should

LYDIA: Let me find you some money

LYDIA fishes in her purse and pulls out two twenty-pound notes.

Forty pounds

She hands it to him.

Thank you.

You know, people like you, people who know how to do stuff, you

You make me feel *possible.*

STEVE: Didn't fix it, did I?

LYDIA: It's not just

Beat. They look at each other.

Um

There's something else I need you to do, would you mind?

STEVE: Um

LYDIA: Just a second.

LYDIA goes to the kitchen. STEVE rubs the back of his head. LYDIA comes back carrying an electric kettle. She puts it on the table between them. STEVE looks at it. Then at LYDIA.

STEVE: I, um

STEVE clears his throat.

I don't do kettles

LYDIA: No. Course not. Stupid.

I'm sorry, I'm trying to

I read a book this week which I really shouldn't do because I get so sad when I get to the end

And

Pause.

STEVE: What's um

What's wrong with it?

LYDIA: Won't boil water

STEVE: Right

LYDIA: Which is actually all I / need it to do

STEVE: Need it to do, yeah

Have you tried the fuse?

LYDIA: Yeah, I can do plugs.

STEVE: You changed it?

LYDIA: Yes

STEVE: You might have to just buy a new one. Argos, or

LYDIA: I know how to buy a kettle.

STEVE: Course.

STEVE swings his backpack onto his back. He has a sudden burst of pain in his hand.

Ah *fuck.*

LYDIA: God, you OK?

STEVE: Yeah, I

LYDIA: Sit down

STEVE: No, I. Shit.

LYDIA: God, can I help can I do anything?

STEVE looks at LYDIA.

Would you like a drink? I mean, go for a drink?

Pause.

STEVE: I, um

227

LYDIA: No. Yeah. No, that was a better idea before you got here, actually. Didn't seem so. I had this idea that maybe

Is your hand OK?

STEVE: Yeah.

LYDIA: I've completely cack-handled this

STEVE: No

LYDIA: Just thought maybe we could go out for a drink.

STEVE: Um, when?

LYDIA: Um, now?

STEVE: OK.

LYDIA: OK.

STEVE holds his hand up.

STEVE: Mine's a pint. With a straw.

LYDIA laughs.

Fade.

SCENE 5

Evening. GREG and HAYLEY are eating dinner in a Chinese restaurant.

GREG is frowning at HAYLEY's drink.

GREG: And that's a drink, is it? *Bubble* tea

HAYLEY: Try a bit?

She offers him her straw.

GREG: Got something floating in the bottom, blob of something

HAYLEY: Tapioca balls

GREG: That supposed to be there?

HAYLEY laughs.

HAYLEY: Yes

They're chewy

Want a bit?

GREG: No I

Drinks with bits in, I don't

HAYLEY: Taste of the future

GREG makes a face and goes back to his noodles. HAYLEY laughs.

Listen thanks for this afternoon, what you said in the meeting

GREG: Well I realise I. I think before I may have made it seem like I thought you didn't know what you were doing

HAYLEY: Yes

GREG: Like I thought you were too young to

HAYLEY: Yes

GREG: And now, having worked with you I realise

I think I was possibly *rude*

HAYLEY: Yes

GREG: Brusque

HAYLEY laughs.

HAYLEY: Good word.

Well thank you.

GREG: Still not convinced by the rest of them

HAYLEY: They'll win you round

GREG: Silly haircuts

HAYLEY: Well the good thing about the rest of them is they all answer to me

GREG: There we go then

HAYLEY: There we go

GREG: Here

GREG takes a small package out of his suit pocket and hands it to HAYLEY. HAYLEY looks at him, questioning.

Little something. Personal

HAYLEY picks up the package and starts to open it.

HAYLEY: I'm intrigued

Thank you

It's a case for her Palm Pilot.

GREG: For your PDA

HAYLEY: Yes. Thank you

GREG: You didn't replace it already

HAYLEY: No

HAYLEY takes her Palm Pilot out of her jacket, which is draped over the back of her chair, and replaces the broken case with the new one.

There we go, look

GREG: Quite snazzy

HAYLEY: Thank you, that was really

Thank you

GREG: Is your hand OK?

HAYLEY: My

GREG: Your hand – you made a face when you took the case off

HAYLEY: Oh

Just a little twinge

GREG: Getting old

HAYLEY: Pulled a muscle or something it's fine

GREG sits back in his chair, looks at HAYLEY. She puts the Palm Pilot into her jacket pocket, smiling.

We can go back to baiting each other now if you like

GREG: Your turn

HAYLEY: We don't have to.

GREG: Would you say you were happy?

HAYLEY: Is that baiting?

GREG: No

HAYLEY: That's a very personal / question

GREG: It's a very simple question

HAYLEY: I don't think

GREG: I'm not violating any kind of code or

I didn't ask what colour knickers you're wearing

Just, are you happy?

GREG's phone rings.

HAYLEY: D'you want to

GREG: No

He looks at the caller display. It's his wife.

God no.

He switches it off.

You married?

HAYLEY: No

GREG: It's hard work

HAYLEY: I'm in a long-term committed / thing

GREG: How long?

HAYLEY: Eight years

GREG: Try twenty-one

You didn't answer my question, are you happy?

HAYLEY: Yes

GREG: Not just OK, not just yes because you're a failure if you're not.

Actually *consciously* happy.

Beat.

HAYLEY: Are you?

GREG: For example – when you walk in, at home

HAYLEY: Yes

GREG: And you see your what, boyfriend, partner?

HAYLEY: Boyfriend

GREG: At the end of the day when you see him, are you happy?

HAYLEY thinks.

HAYLEY: Yes.

Yes I'm always happy to see him

It's just sometimes I'm pretending.

GREG: Oh yes. That one

HAYLEY: Yeah?

HAYLEY picks up some food with her chopsticks but drops it half way to her mouth.

Not very um, dextrous today

GREG: Shall we get you a fork?

HAYLEY: Yeah.

They look around for the waiter. GREG sees him across the room and tries to catch his eye but fails.

GREG: Ever feel like you're being ignored?

HAYLEY smiles.

Probably scared I want to complain about the bits in your drink

He gets up.

HAYLEY: Greg / it's fine

GREG: Not a problem

GREG goes to find a fork. HAYLEY watches him go, then takes her Palm Pilot out of her jacket pocket and looks at it, smiling. She sees GREG returning and replaces it hurriedly, knocking her jacket off the back of the chair as she turns round. GREG sits down and hands her a fork.

HAYLEY: Thank you

GREG: So not happy

HAYLEY: Oh

I don't know

GREG: Hang on your jacket's

GREG stands and picks the jacket up, then puts it on the back of HAYLEY's chair carefully.

Tell me about him

HAYLEY: It's not

Yes it is about him. Probably.

HAYLEY picks up her fork and starts to eat.

God, that's better. That's easier

Last week I

Last week for the first time I noticed the noise he makes
when he kisses me

GREG: Fatal

HAYLEY: And you know he'd never, like just now with my
jacket he'd never do that. Wouldn't even notice. And I
think maybe I want someone who

Just the watching out the uncalled-for little things like that

But I can't just say, can I? That I'd love him more if he
carried my bag I mean what does that sound like?

I mean even to me it sounds

And anyway once you've *asked* it's not

GREG: Yes

HAYLEY: And I don't know when I started to think like that,
like a few years ago I

It's like I'm changing but not *actually* you know there's no
actual or circumstantial

Just things I think changing. The way I think

Like the other day I'm on the train to Slough or
Maidenhead or

GREG: Somewhere fun

HAYLEY: And I bought the paper and I read this article about
um, tiger prawns, did you know this?

GREG: No

HAYLEY: Tiger prawn farming it's like, it's this really big problem it's apparently it destroys the land, the the the *mangroves* in Vietnam and Thailand and places like that they cut all the mangroves down so they can farm these shrimp. But then the chemicals and stuff they feed to them because of that level of acid or whatever going into the soil it kills it, the um the earth is after a few years it's worthless it's completely spent so when the shrimp farming fails, when all the shrimp die which apparently happens quite a lot or the crop gets contaminated or whatever, they can't go back to farming anything else. But no-one tells them that so all this land gets used up 'cause demand's got so big and everyone wants all these poor farmers to grow tiger prawns not rice or whatever so the economy's going to shit in these countries because we all like tiger prawns so much

GREG: I don't really like prawns

HAYLEY: OK well

GREG: Carry on

HAYLEY: So I read this in the morning and then by about eleven when I'm starting to get hungry for lunch all I can think about is fucking tiger prawns, how much I want a tiger prawn sandwich so I'm scouring Marks and Spencers in Slough or

GREG: Maidenhead or

HAYLEY: Somewhere bollocks and I'm just absolutely desperate for a tiger prawn salad you know. After reading that. And I think what does that

And then I'm not sure if I care

Like fox hunting

Like I know I'm I'm opposed to fox hunting I know I must be I just

I can't remember why

GREG: OK

HAYLEY: And sometimes you know, sometimes I think I'd
really like to *wear fur*

Pause. GREG laughs.

For example.

HAYLEY laughs.

GREG: You're brilliant

HAYLEY: Am I?

GREG: I think so

I do, you're so

HAYLEY: I'm just permanently I don't know *baffled*

GREG: Good word

HAYLEY: I'm thirty already, you know?

GREG: Well, *thirty*

HAYLEY: I mean I don't think it's like an age crisis just. You
know, *thirty*

GREG: But everyone feels like that, don't they? Whatever age

HAYLEY: Do they?

HAYLEY sits back in her chair.

So what are they doing, are they all just coping?

GREG: I suppose.

HAYLEY: It's commonplace

GREG: I'm not saying you're not having a difficult

HAYLEY: Happens all the time

GREG: You don't

People like you don't

Don't happen all the time.

Fade.

SCENE 6

Putney High Street, 1:00 AM.

STEVE is moving away from a cashpoint, clumsily trying to slide some notes into his wallet. He's in the middle of telling LYDIA a story. LYDIA stands a few paces off, listening to STEVE, a little wobbly. They're having a nice time.

STEVE: So basically by then she's so desperate she tells me, like right in the middle of this open-plan office, she tells me if I can get the file back she'll not only love me forever she'll also take me out for dinner that night

LYDIA: And you did

STEVE: You know, I'm sat there thinking if I can string this out a bit longer she'll offer me a blow job

LYDIA giggles.

I got the file back, yeah

Tried to make it look a bit difficult, you know, but it's just sat there in the Recycle Bin

Anyway she did take me for dinner and she was so relieved about the file she got a bit drunk and we accidentally ended up shagging and then here we are

Eight years later.

Beat.

LYDIA: Four five seven nine

STEVE: What?

LYDIA: Four five seven nine

STEVE: D'you want to shout it a bit louder?

LYDIA: Sorry

LYDIA giggles.

Sorry

All that forty pounds just on drinks

She sees he's still having trouble with the money.

You alright there?

STEVE: Yeah, I

LYDIA: Here

She takes the wallet and slides the cash into it for him.

I'm not going to nick it

What is it, arthritis or

STEVE: You looked over my shoulder

LYDIA hands the wallet back.

LYDIA: Can't help it

STEVE: You're not supposed to look, it's

LYDIA: I don't usually tell people

STEVE: But you usually look?

LYDIA: Can't help it

She staggers slightly.

God, I'm a bit

Nice that bar, isn't it?

STEVE: Yeah

LYDIA: Will you be in trouble?

STEVE: What?

LYDIA: At home, being home so late. Missing the last tube

STEVE: She'll be asleep. Might not notice

STEVE looks back at the cashpoint.

LYDIA: What is it?

STEVE: I'll have to change it now

LYDIA: Change what?

STEVE: PIN number

LYDIA: Oh come on

STEVE: You might tell someone

LYDIA: I won't

STEVE: No offence but I'd feel a bit

LYDIA: You won't change it because it's the same PIN number you've had since forever and there isn't another four digits in the world you'd trust yourself to remember without having to write it down. Right?

God I'm actually

STEVE: What?

LYDIA: You stopped being laid-back for a second there

Beat.

STEVE: I should grab a taxi

LYDIA: Can I get in it with you?

Drop me home

STEVE: OK

LYDIA: Stop me from shouting your PIN number in the street, won't it?

STEVE looks around for a taxi.

D'you have a joint account, you and Hayley?

STEVE: Yeah

LYDIA: Do you?

STEVE: Yeah. Not for, not for everything.

I mean, this wasn't

LYDIA: No. What d'you use it for?

STEVE: Joint things, the flat, bills, that stuff

LYDIA: You don't pay your income into it?

STEVE: Uh-uh. She earns a fuckload more than me, so

LYDIA: D'you think you'll stay together, you two?

STEVE: Never know, do you?

STEVE puts his hand out for a taxi, which sails past.

Shit

LYDIA sits down on the kerb.

LYDIA: If you could be more something, what would it be?

STEVE: More

LYDIA: You know like more intelligent, more rich more happy

STEVE: More

More, um

I don't know, more

LYDIA: Articulate?

LYDIA laughs.

Sorry

STEVE thinks.

There must be something, some ambition, something you want

STEVE: Um

LYDIA: Or like something you had and you'd like it back, something you used to do that doesn't happen anymore

LYDIA looks at STEVE, then away.

I used to dance, years ago

STEVE: Yeah?

LYDIA: I mean, I used to go to places like clubs and. Places where you dance. And now I don't even go to those places and even if I did I probably wouldn't dance now

LYDIA stands.

Is she. Is it everything you've ever wanted?

STEVE: It's fine

LYDIA: Fuck Steve, it's *fine*?

STEVE: You just

LYDIA: What?

STEVE: I don't know you get to a stage where it's all OK, you know it just carries on and it's OK

LYDIA: Which is exactly what you want a life that's *OK*

STEVE walks away a few paces.

I'm sorry I've been

I mean I realise I am I realise I can be a little bit *irritating*

STEVE: No

LYDIA: That would be my 'less' thing. Less irritating

I um. I haven't been out of the house in a week. So I'm a bit giddy. And I don't usually drink alcohol at home 'cause drinking on your own's so

Actually, I'm lying, I have been out – on Tuesday I went to the supermarket down the road with my sunglasses on at like seven at night. Oh, and then on Thursday I got so fed up with my own company I just left the flat, like when people have an argument and one of them just walks out of the house and slams the door I wanted to be that person. But then I was on the street and I didn't really have anywhere to go and no-one to go back into the house and hug sorry so I went to the newsagents to fucking *browse*

LYDIA looks at STEVE. He's clutching his hand and wincing.

You alright?

STEVE: Not brilliant

LYDIA: Get you a taxi

She looks around. There aren't any. Looks back at STEVE.

Oh, you poor thing

She puts her hands around his and strokes them.

STEVE: What would you be more of, what's your 'more' thing?

LYDIA: Oh, um. More brave. Braver

STEVE: Yeah

LYDIA looks away, then at STEVE. She takes his hand and plants a slow kiss on his palm. She looks up at him.

Sorry, my wrist

LYDIA smiles and goes to kiss the inside of his wrist. STEVE takes his hand away.

No, I mean. Ow. Sorry, it hurts

LYDIA: Sorry

STEVE: Sometimes they're numb or they tingle or

They're tingling, like they're *full* of something it's so

LYDIA: It's got cold, you should probably keep it warm

LYDIA takes her scarf and wraps it around STEVE's hands. She takes a piece of paper from her pocket.

I've um. This is my phone number

She puts the piece of paper in his pocket.

Just, you know. Since I've nothing else for you to fix

She looks around for a taxi.

Fade.

SCENE 7

HAYLEY and STEVE's flat. Late morning.

STEVE is sitting at the kitchen counter eating a yoghurt through a straw. He isn't holding the pot, so it skids a little on the work surface. HAYLEY watches him, holding a pile of leaflets.

HAYLEY: So there's lots of things it could be, they gave me all these

    She lays the leaflets out on the counter.

    Repetitive Strain Injury, apparently it's usually some kind of repeated action, not always it doesn't have to be that

    As STEVE gets to the bottom of the yoghurt pot the straw makes a slurping noise.

    There's lots of different sorts

    Carpal Tunnel Syndrome

    Rheumatoid arthritis

STEVE: You took the morning off

HAYLEY: Tendinitis

STEVE: To go to the doctor for me?

HAYLEY: Tenosynovitis

    You weren't going to do it

    Tennis elbow

    Your elbows are fine, aren't they?

STEVE: Just my hands

    STEVE slurps the yoghurt again. HAYLEY frowns. She snatches the pot away from him, cuffing one of his hands as she does so.

Ow

STEVE holds his wrist.

HAYLEY: I didn't do that.

STEVE: Sudden movement it

HAYLEY puts the pot in the bin.

Ow

HAYLEY: Oh, look

Holds a leaflet towards STEVE.

Potential risks of computer games and text messaging, there
you go.

STEVE: You didn't have to go for me

HAYLEY: I know

Must be love

And you won't take the herbal things I got

STEVE sits down.

The symptoms are kind of the same for most of them so

You look at the treatment rather than the cause, apparently

STEVE: What's the treatment?

HAYLEY: Um, keeping still

You'll be alright there / then

STEVE: Keeping still, that's it?

HAYLEY: Ice-packs make it hurt less

STEVE: Right

HAYLEY: And you mustn't let it get too hot or that makes it swell up more

STEVE: Ah

HAYLEY: What?

STEVE: Been keeping it warm

HAYLEY: You see this is why you should have

(*Mimicking her 'nagging' voice.*) nya nya nya

STEVE: What else?

HAYLEY: Anti-inflammatory drugs, Nurofen, ibuprofen stuff

STEVE: Not strong enough I've been / taking them

HAYLEY: You've

You didn't tell me

STEVE: Just 'cause I didn't tell you doesn't mean I'm not doing anything

Don't work anyway

HAYLEY: Well you can get stronger ones from the doctor

HAYLEY hands him a pharmacy package.

Like these

Thank you, Hayley

STEVE doesn't take them.

It's this or cortisone shots and I'm not doing that for you I hate needles

HAYLEY swaps the package from one hand to the other, wincing slightly. STEVE frowns.

STEVE: How'd you get a prescription?

HAYLEY puts the package down.

HAYLEY: Begged and pleaded

Must be love

STEVE: Hayley

HAYLEY: What?

STEVE: You can't have got a prescription for me, surely

HAYLEY: Maybe I shagged the doctor

I got ice-packs

HAYLEY takes four ice-packs out of a plastic bag.

STEVE: Only got two hands

HAYLEY: Two to use and two to keep in the freezer, isn't it?

They're not ice right now, obviously, they have to go in the freezer for a bit so

HAYLEY pulls the freezer door open. She winces and holds her wrist.

Tsss

STEVE looks at her.

Fine

Beat.

Fine. Probably just sympathy pain

HAYLEY closes the freezer door with her hip. She meets STEVE's eye.

So I've got sympathy twinges.

STEVE: Is it both?

HAYLEY: Right one's worse

STEVE: Fingers or

HAYLEY: Fingers, wrist

STEVE: Shit

HAYLEY: I didn't get it to piss you off

I'll just take a couple of days sick, rest up

It's been stressful so

STEVE: Work

HAYLEY: Yeah, did you notice?

What?

STEVE: You didn't actually take the morning off for me, then

HAYLEY: Well no I

No.

HAYLEY goes to sit on the sofa.

STEVE stands looking at her, then around the room, unnerved at having her there during the day. HAYLEY sits on the sofa looking ahead, her hands in her lap.

STEVE: So you're just going to

HAYLEY: Waiting for the ice-packs

STEVE: Right

HAYLEY: That alright with you?

STEVE: Course

HAYLEY: Anything you'd like to say? While we're here?

STEVE: I don't know, sorry?

HAYLEY: It's not your fault it's not bloody infectious is it?

Beat.

D'you want any lunch?

STEVE: No

HAYLEY: Because I can't be bothered to / make any

STEVE: I had some. Didn't think you'd be here

HAYLEY: What did you have?

STEVE: Soup

HAYLEY: God, Steve

D'you know what's happening?

STEVE: No

STEVE goes to sit on the sofa next to HAYLEY.

HAYLEY: You don't have to

STEVE: What?

HAYLEY: Nothing it's fine

They both look ahead.

STEVE: So what's your repeated action, then?

HAYLEY: I don't know, repetitive strain of putting up with you?

STEVE: Don't say that, kiss me

HAYLEY looks at STEVE.

What?

HAYLEY: I don't tingle anymore

I used to

To tingle

STEVE: My hands tingle

HAYLEY: Yeah, my hands tingle just not

Everything I feel feels like it's in my hands

Rest of me's totally

STEVE: Numb

HAYLEY: You know, when we first started you were the sun on my face

STEVE: Kiss me

HAYLEY: Now the sun is the sun on my face

Beat.

Fucking hurts, doesn't it?

Fade.

SCENE 8

LYDIA's studio flat. Late morning.

STEVE and LYDIA face each other. There are no objects between them.

STEVE: I thought maybe, you know

   Maybe you might need some help with your toaster

LYDIA: No, toaster's fine

STEVE: Or the dishwasher or

LYDIA: Haven't got one

STEVE: Right

   OK

LYDIA: It's all fine

STEVE: Did I

LYDIA: What?

STEVE: Have I done something wrong?

LYDIA: No. No

   Just

   Surprised to see you

   Haven't seen you in, what

STEVE: Don't know

LYDIA: Three weeks

   Something like that

STEVE: / Sorry

LYDIA: No, it's fine, how are you?

253

STEVE: I'd have come sooner but

  I've been really

  Can't do anything, can't ride my bike I walked here today

LYDIA: And your phone's been cut off

STEVE: No, it

LYDIA: Joking, just a joke

STEVE: The keys are hard, the buttons

LYDIA: Right

STEVE: Had to completely stop typing, can't work at all

LYDIA: God, that's

  I'm really sorry

STEVE: No

  LYDIA smiles.

LYDIA: Nice to see you

  As usual

STEVE: Yeah

LYDIA: I wasn't sure if I would

STEVE: No?

LYDIA: After, you know, after

  You know

  You kind of disappeared a bit

STEVE: Sorry

LYDIA: No, I'm

STEVE is cradling his left hand.

Are they hurting?

STEVE: Bit

LYDIA: Would it

Can I help keep them warm?

STEVE: No

LYDIA: No

STEVE: Not because

LYDIA: No?

STEVE: 'Cause it turns out cold is better. Ice-packs and

LYDIA: Right. Should've taken more notice in Biology

STEVE: They wouldn't have taught

LYDIA: No I suppose not

STEVE: At that level

Pause. They're standing very close.

LYDIA: I've got ice in the freezer or peas or

STEVE: OK

LYDIA: OK.

LYDIA goes to the freezer and takes out a packet of frozen peas.

These are in a packet so. Keeps it contained not like ice in a plastic bag rattling around, leaking and

Which one, is it both or

STEVE: Yeah

LYDIA: I've only got the one

STEVE: This one's worse

LYDIA: OK

She applies the packet to STEVE's left hand.

STEVE: I don't want to

LYDIA: What?

STEVE: Make them go bad, melt and

LYDIA: I never eat peas it's fine. Don't know why I've got them. I've got a tin of beans as well somewhere, never going to eat it. Coconut milk in a can I mean I wouldn't know where to start you know?

That better?

STEVE: Yeah.

LYDIA takes STEVE's right hand and uses it to hold the packet in place. She moves away, laughs a little.

What?

LYDIA: I kind of missed you

STEVE: Yeah?

LYDIA: Funny how someone can

People get important, you know?

STEVE: Um

LYDIA: Then they go away

STEVE: I should've

I didn't realise

LYDIA: No, that's

No reason why you would

I don't have many people around so I get a bit silly about people

STEVE: Right

LYDIA: And quite often I frighten them off

STEVE: OK

LYDIA: So I thought I might have frightened you off

And you probably don't you probably don't need anyone and

I mean god knows what I'd *add*

STEVE: I wasn't frightened I was just

LYDIA: Poorly, yeah

Sorry I'm just

Kind of explaining how I get silly about

I mean when you came in today when I opened the door I had this *physical*

Beat.

I had such a lovely time the other week. When we went out.

STEVE: Me too

STEVE looks away.

LYDIA: Are you OK?

STEVE: Yeah, I

LYDIA: Something wrong?

STEVE: Things are a bit

At home

LYDIA: D'you want to tell me?

STEVE shakes his head, still looking away. Pause.

D'you know what would be OK?

STEVE: What?

LYDIA: If you'd come round because

Because you kind of needed a hug

Beat.

That would make me really happy you know, if

If you'd needed a hug and you'd come to me

Pause.

STEVE: I

LYDIA: Doesn't matter

How's your hand?

STEVE: I don't know what to

LYDIA: We could just forget I said anything

STEVE sits down on the bed. He puts his head in his hands.

STEVE: Ow

LYDIA looks at the frozen peas.

LYDIA: That's probably defrosting now I should probably

She sits down by STEVE and takes the packet from his hand.

STEVE: I did

LYDIA: Did what?

STEVE: Because I needed a hug

LYDIA: You don't have to say that

> *STEVE looks away again.*

> Steve

> Oh

> *LYDIA goes to put her arms around STEVE.*

STEVE: But gently 'cause I do really hurt

> *LYDIA strokes his back.*

LYDIA: How's that?

STEVE: Yeah

LYDIA: Lie down

> Come on you need to

> I won't kiss any of you and if you happen to cry I won't say anything

> *STEVE lies on his side on the bed, his hands in front of his face.*

STEVE: They look weird, wrong, they look like someone else's

LYDIA: Shh

> *LYDIA strokes his hair.*

> How's that?

STEVE: Yeah

> I could sleep

LYDIA: I like that

STEVE closes his eyes. LYDIA lies down behind him and continues to hold him. The room darkens as STEVE falls asleep, until it is lit only by the blue light from the computer screen. A moment of painless quiet.

LYDIA carefully sits up. She looks at STEVE and smiles. She looks over at the computer. She gets off the bed carefully and creeps over to sit at the computer. She types a couple of words then looks over to check if it has woken STEVE. It hasn't. STEVE starts to snore. LYDIA giggles to herself. She goes back to the screen and types quickly, checks what she's written and is satisfied. She switches on the printer. It makes a succession of scraping and scratching noises as it calibrates.

Dammit.

LYDIA tries to switch it off, but it won't oblige.

Shut up shut up. Shh

STEVE wakes up and the room is fully light again. LYDIA turns to see him.

Sorry. I'm sorry

It's new I'd forgotten it makes such a noise

STEVE: 'S OK

STEVE sits up, accidentally leans on his hand as he does so.

Ow

LYDIA: Ooh

OK?

STEVE: Yeah

LYDIA: I didn't mean to wake you, sorry

STEVE: What you doing?

LYDIA: Job application

Sudden burst of energy

Last day for getting it in today and it looks like it might be perfect so

STEVE rubs his eyes.

Turns out you snore

STEVE: Yeah

LYDIA: I'm a light sleeper

LYDIA turns back to the computer.

I'm going to say I used this five months to improve my computer skills. So it doesn't seem such a big gap. Teach myself all the stuff, spreadsheets and

STEVE looks at the printer.

STEVE: Nice printer

LYDIA: Yeah

STEVE: You installed it

LYDIA: No. That um, superstore place. They send a chap round with the delivery. Really helpful.

STEVE stands up, awkward.

STEVE: Cool

LYDIA: Are you embarrassed?

STEVE: No

LYDIA: 'Cause you fell asleep

STEVE: No, not

STEVE sits back down on the bed.

Just now I had this, I've had it before but lying here I had this

The toaster was

LYDIA: The toaster?

STEVE: Yeah

LYDIA: My toaster?

STEVE: No, mine at home it

LYDIA: This is a dream?

STEVE: Yeah. Yeah

Whenever I put anything in it it disappeared out the bottom

Not onto the floor or

Like there was some kind of black hole, an abyss or something.

Beat.

LYDIA: Let me take you home

STEVE: Take me home

LYDIA: Yes

STEVE: I'm not sure I

LYDIA: You need looking after

Not medically, just

STEVE: I don't want to go home

LYDIA: You've kind of got to go home, Steve. It's where you live

I'll look after you.

Fade.

SCENE 9

Coffee bar. Early afternoon.

GREG and HAYLEY sit facing each other. He has a cappuccino, she has an iced coffee with a straw. They smile at each other, easy.

HAYLEY: Did you know infinity's not the biggest thing anymore?

GREG: No

HAYLEY: They found something bigger

GREG: What?

HAYLEY: Don't know

It was on the train last week, going to Slough or

GREG: Swindon or

HAYLEY: Somewhere fun. And there's some bloke opposite me reading the New Scientist or something and on the front the headline was 'Infinity – not the biggest thing'.

Makes you think, doesn't it?

GREG: Yeah.

HAYLEY: Made me laugh. And I thought about telling you when I saw it, I sort of turned to you as if you were (*She gestures to the space beside her.*)

I wanted to tell you.

So we should get back to the office, really

GREG: You wouldn't like to sit here flirting a bit longer?

HAYLEY: Would you?

GREG: Give me your hand

HAYLEY: I can't

GREG: Why?

HAYLEY: Hurts to move it

GREG: Alright

    Imagine I'm holding your hand

HAYLEY: OK

    That's

    Surprisingly nice

GREG: Surprisingly?

HAYLEY: Nice surprise, I mean

GREG: You like it

HAYLEY: Yeah

GREG: Good

    GREG sits back in his chair.

    Side of your nose

HAYLEY: Greg

GREG: Tell me that isn't nice

HAYLEY: It's

GREG: Surprisingly nice

HAYLEY: Yeah

GREG: Which side?

    HAYLEY closes her eyes, tilts her head to the left slightly.

HAYLEY: That side

GREG: There

Where now?

HAYLEY tilts her head the other way.

HAYLEY: That side

GREG: Yes

There.

HAYLEY leans forward.

HAYLEY: What else?

GREG: Your bottom lip

HAYLEY: God

GREG: I want to…suck your bottom lip

HAYLEY: God

GREG: Too much?

HAYLEY: I

No, not too much

GREG: Sure?

HAYLEY: Just

New

Feels different

Beat.

GREG: Hot, isn't it?

GREG smiles.

HAYLEY: Your face, you're so naughty

GREG: I want to I want to suck your finger

Each one of them in turn and lick the palm of your hand and a line up your arm, pushing your sleeve back a little and lick the inside of your elbow

And I want to put my hand on your stomach, touch your skin

HAYLEY: God

GREG: And

No, your turn

Beat.

HAYLEY: OK, I

I'm not very

GREG: Go on

HAYLEY: OK

I want to…run my fingers through the short hair at the back of your neck

GREG: Uh-huh

HAYLEY: Starched line of your shirt collar

And

And slide my hands around your waist, underneath your jacket

Untuck your shirt at the back, run my fingers along

GREG: I want to put my tongue through the holes between the buttons in your shirt

LAURA WADE

HAYLEY: And you do these tiny little kisses down the side of
my neck

GREG: I want to stand behind you, holding you close round
your waist so you feel me hard against your arse

HAYLEY: All the time with these tiny little kisses

GREG: And I want to undo the buttons on your shirt, slide it
off your shoulders

HAYLEY: Facing me, your eyes and my eyes and your hands in
the back of my hair

GREG: And bite your shoulder

HAYLEY: Bite my shoulder?

GREG: Gently. It'll be nice

HAYLEY: Your hands in the back of my hair and stroking my
hair

Pulling me to you

GREG: And then undo the button on your trousers and slide the
zip down

HAYLEY: Your hands either side of my face

GREG: Slide my hand inside

HAYLEY: Kissing my eyelids

GREG: Before you expect me to

Make you shiver with the surprise

Slide my hand into your pants

HAYLEY: Knickers. God, are we at knickers already?

GREG: I don't know, are we?

HAYLEY looks at GREG, thinking. A moment. She bends down slowly to take a sip of her iced coffee. GREG watches her.

Christ, even when you

Just watching you drink coffee makes me

HAYLEY looks away.

Are you

HAYLEY looks at GREG.

HAYLEY: Put your hand inside

GREG: Inside your knickers?

HAYLEY: Do it

GREG: OK. Sliding my hand inside

HAYLEY: Yeah

GREG: My finger between your legs into your cunt

HAYLEY: Pussy

GREG: Your pussy

HAYLEY: Are you happy with pussy? I don't like cunt

GREG: Pussy

And your hands around my

HAYLEY: Dick

GREG: Really?

HAYLEY: What d'you prefer?

GREG: Cock, I always think

HAYLEY: I always think cock sounds a bit gay

Beat.

GREG: Little bit of sweat on your forehead

HAYLEY: And I pull you into me

GREG: Already?

HAYLEY: I want you in me

GREG: I won't last long

HAYLEY: Want to feel you that close to me

I don't mind if you don't last long

GREG: Push into you harder and harder

HAYLEY: Slowly

But really deep

GREG: My head against your shoulder

HAYLEY: Looking into my eyes and we're moving and our eyes are *locked*

GREG: And you feel it

You feel it

You really feel like you're being *fucked*

HAYLEY: Fuck

GREG: What?

HAYLEY: I

GREG: What?

HAYLEY: No, carry on

GREG: What's wrong?

HAYLEY: Don't stop now Greg, you're so close

GREG: You're crying

HAYLEY: I'm not crying

GREG: What is it?

HAYLEY: I'm not crying

    I

GREG: What?

HAYLEY: I feel like I'm really being *fucked*

GREG: Let's go somewhere

HAYLEY: What?

GREG: Let's go somewhere

    A hotel or

HAYLEY: Greg

GREG: Yes

HAYLEY: I'm crying

GREG: Yes

HAYLEY: I started crying and you want to take me to a hotel

    Beat.

    Greg I can't

GREG: I know

HAYLEY: *You* can't

GREG: You know, we both can

HAYLEY: Yes I know

271

GREG: D'you want to?

HAYLEY: I'm crying

GREG: Because you want to or because you don't want to?

HAYLEY: I don't know

GREG sits back in his chair.

GREG: You don't know.

HAYLEY looks away.

HAYLEY: You know I've been having this thing

GREG: Yes

HAYLEY: These thoughts about maybe

You know

HAYLEY looks at her lap.

But

It's like

I don't know, like I thought I could just go for a little walk

Just a little wander around, look at stuff, the scenery

GREG: Men

HAYLEY: Other men yes

GREG: The the grass is / greener

HAYLEY: Oh my god the grass isn't just greener I mean it's got ten-foot sunflowers I can I can *smell* them if sunflowers smell, I don't know

GREG: Right

HAYLEY: I mean it's almost it's almost unbearable being able to smell it and all because of the

The stupid walk, just this thinky little walk looking at the scenery 'cause when I started I just wandered around a little while and it was fine it was pleasant I could see stuff and then

Because all of a sudden I realised I'd actually wandered to the top of a cliff

Like the walk up to it had been like this, really flat

She gestures to demonstrate the gradual incline of the hill then clutches her arm.

Tss. Twinge, sorry

Sorry

So it's pretty flat really only a little bit of a hill then all of a sudden I get to the edge of this cliff and there's water below it and I'm standing looking down at these waves and I'd never meant to be there I'd just gone for this thinky little walk

And some of me's thinking god, this is interesting I mean most of me's terrified but a lot of me's thinking bloody hell this is interesting

You know?

GREG: And what happens next in the dream, do you

HAYLEY: It's not a dream it's a metaphor it's

I'm contemplating jumping

GREG: Really?

HAYLEY: Yeah. Because it looks good and exciting down there and

But then I start to worry I'll stand too close to the edge, I'll stand on a piece of loose rock and it'll crumble and I'll lose my footing and then I'll fall. Because of standing too close and thinking about it.

And then – what? I'm in the sea and there's no ladder back up and this is assuming the fall and the impact hasn't killed me or I haven't landed on a rock or something but what if I can't climb up?

GREG: You don't have to climb back up.

HAYLEY: But I can't just

Greg, I can't swim

I can't do it.

I'm sorry.

Fade.

SCENE 10

Kitchen/Living Room area of HAYLEY and STEVE's flat. Afternoon.

LYDIA sits on the kitchen counter, her legs crossed. STEVE sits on a stool, his arms on the counter, bent, his hands starting to claw. There's a plastic bowl beside them full of nearly-melted ice-lollies.

LYDIA: So I'm standing in the kitchen this morning making a cup of tea and the freezer it. It audibly exhaled, like it let out this long sigh

Like it was breathing

STEVE: Sigh of relief

LYDIA: Dunno

STEVE: (*The lolly-sticks.*) How they doing?

LYDIA: Nearly melted

LYDIA lifts a stick out of the bowl.

Yeah, some of these are done

She puts the stick back and licks her fingers.

Bit sticky, have to give them a wipe

I couldn't think of anything but lolly-sticks that'd work

STEVE: No

LYDIA: And then I tried to think where I could buy the sticks without lollies on them and

STEVE: Not obvious

LYDIA: I couldn't think of anywhere.

And I've no idea how we get them attached to your fingers

STEVE: Bandages

The front door slams, off.

LYDIA: Is that

STEVE: (*Calling.*) Hayley?

STEVE looks at LYDIA.

LYDIA: Just introduce me, it's fine

HAYLEY comes into the kitchen. She leans on the doorframe.

STEVE: You alright?

HAYLEY: Yeah fine who's this?

STEVE: This is my friend Lydia

HAYLEY: Hi

LYDIA: Hi, nice to meet / you

HAYLEY: How d'you guys

LYDIA: Steve fixes my computer I'm hopeless

HAYLEY: Are you sleeping with her?

STEVE: Am I

HAYLEY: Sleeping with her

STEVE looks at LYDIA.

Are you having sex with her?

STEVE: Oh no, No

HAYLEY: Steve's clients often try to have sex with him

STEVE: No they

HAYLEY: The women

Most of your clients are hopeless women, aren't they?

STEVE: Some of them

HAYLEY: He's an absolute godsend

LYDIA: I don't want to sleep with him

HAYLEY: No, I wouldn't recommend it. Not 'cause I'd punch you or anything just 'cause he's cr

STEVE: Hayley

Pause.

Are you pissed?

HAYLEY: Apparently you know, apparently if you drink fizzy alcohol through a straw it makes you more drunk

Which, you know, which is some consolation

STEVE: It's half past four

HAYLEY: Pubs are open.

(*To LYDIA.*) Did he tell you he's given me RSI?

Sorry, not RSI, I think mine's Carpal Tunnel Syndrome d'you know what that is? The big nerve gets *squeezed*

HAYLEY looks at STEVE.

Injury or over-use

(*Looks at the bowl.*) Oh you made orange soup

LYDIA: Melted um

HAYLEY: It's what?

LYDIA: Melted ice-lollies

HAYLEY: Is it

Why?

277

No, I don't care actually

LYDIA: We were going to make a splint for Steve's hand

HAYLEY: A splint. Marvellous

STEVE: Why you home?

HAYLEY: I'm sick I don't have to work if I'm ill

I'm going to have a drink I think

STEVE: Hayley

HAYLEY: I'm going to have some milk if there is any is there any milk Steve?

STEVE: Yes I th

HAYLEY: Marvellous

HAYLEY opens the fridge door using a strap. She takes out an unopened carton of milk.

Ooh a new one good behaviour what have you done?

STEVE: Nothing

HAYLEY tries to open the carton without success.

HAYLEY: Ow fuck

Can't get this fucker / open now

LYDIA: Here

LYDIA takes the carton and opens it for HAYLEY.

HAYLEY: Ooh she's good isn't she good?

See why you like her, darling, Mrs Fixit.

HAYLEY looks at LYDIA.

I know you

LYDIA: Do / you

HAYLEY: How do I know you?

LYDIA: I don't

HAYLEY: I definitely recognise you

LYDIA: I don't think

HAYLEY: You look so

LYDIA: Just one of those faces, I think

HAYLEY: No, I'm sure I

HAYLEY looks at the sink.

You did the washing up

STEVE: Lydia did it

HAYLEY: Did she now

LYDIA: Sorry, I

Someone once came and did my washing up once when I had flu and it was nice so

HAYLEY: Did Steve do it

LYDIA: Steve

HAYLEY: Your washing up

LYDIA: No. Not Steve

HAYLEY: No. Wouldn't have been Steve.

Pause.

LYDIA: (*To STEVE.*) I should go

HAYLEY: No no no, in my own house, I'll do the going

I am going to another room

She turns to go. Turns back.

With

The milk

She picks up the carton of milk in both hands and goes out of the door. STEVE looks at LYDIA.

STEVE: She's not like that, she's never like that

LYDIA: I'm. I'm going to go

STEVE: You don't have to

LYDIA: Come on, I'm in the way

STEVE: Please

Beat.

LYDIA: I do know her

Beat.

The job I had

Hayley was one of the consultants who decided I probably shouldn't have a job

STEVE: Shit

I'm sorry

LYDIA: No it's fine

I probably wouldn't remember me either

STEVE: I'll talk to her

LYDIA: It's done now

    It was months ago, she

    There's other stuff you need to sort out, Steve

    You need to do something

STEVE: Don't go

    STEVE leans in to LYDIA, tries to kiss her. She backs away.

LYDIA: N

    No

    Steve

STEVE: Sorry

LYDIA: No

    Beat.

    You do need to do something I don't think it's *that*

    Starting some stupid thing with me isn't

    LYDIA looks away, then looks around the room.

    You told me Hayley likes air-fresheners

STEVE: Yeah

LYDIA: I think they must have all run out 'cause it smells Steve

STEVE: It smells

LYDIA: Stinks. Coming in from outside

    LYDIA bites her lip.

    That was ridiculous what you just did

STEVE: Sorry

LYDIA: I should

I should just walk away

STEVE: I'm sorry. I'm sorry

LYDIA: You need to talk to her

STEVE: I'm crap at

LYDIA: You need to sort it out

STEVE: I know. I'm crap

LYDIA: No, Steve, you can't just

You can't just say that and be crap

It's not enough to just identify that you're crap and then always be that, you know?

I'll call in a couple of days, OK?

STEVE: OK

LYDIA: OK.

LYDIA leaves. STEVE goes to the kitchen cupboard, which he opens by using a strap around the handle, and takes out an aerosol can of air-freshener. He frowns, trying to work out how he can operate the can with his physically impaired hands. He solves it by placing the can on a surface and pressing the spray button with the flat of his hand. He starts to move around the room, spraying the air, upholstery etc. HAYLEY comes in and leans on the doorframe, slightly sobered up. She watches him.

HAYLEY: She gone, your little friend?

STEVE: Yeah.

STEVE looks at HAYLEY.

HAYLEY: You going to tell me off for drinking all the milk?

STEVE: D'you feel bad?

HAYLEY: Not really.

STEVE sprays.

STEVE: She lost her job.

HAYLEY coughs.

HAYLEY: You trying to as

You trying to asphyxiate me with that?

STEVE: Smells in here

HAYLEY: Why don't we just open the window?

STEVE looks at HAYLEY.

What?

STEVE: She lost her job 'cause of you.

HAYLEY: Can we just

STEVE: Did you hear me?

HAYLEY: Steve, the window?

STEVE: I can't open it I can't turn the catch

You sacked her

HAYLEY: I didn't sack her I don't

We don't say 'sack' it's not

HAYLEY remembers.

Ohhhh

Ohhh *her*

God, yeah, god that company was a mess I *knew* I recognised her

STEVE is looking at her.

What?

STEVE: D'you feel bad? At all?

HAYLEY: Steve

STEVE: You didn't even remember

HAYLEY: It was months ago, project before last

STEVE: She went on holiday and when she got back

HAYLEY: Has she got a new job?

STEVE: No

HAYLEY: No efficiency

STEVE: Takes more than / efficiency to

HAYLEY: Yes it takes a bit of fucking gumption

Look at you, all sorry for her

STEVE: I don't think it's right

HAYLEY: No, well

STEVE: Or fair

HAYLEY: Oh no, definitely not fair

Not fair that I get to be the evil one either

STEVE: I don't think

HAYLEY: That your loyalty or whatever the fuck

That you would assume that I'm the

STEVE: I'm not saying

HAYLEY: And can I just point out while we're at it that the proceeds of my wicked life are going a fair way to funding your completely ineffectual one right now and I haven't heard the slightest bleat of dissent about it from you before?

STEVE: My friend lost her job 'cause of you I'm feeling a bit

HAYLEY: People lose their jobs 'cause of me all the time, you just never met one before.

What d'you want me to do about it? Apart from kill myself.

STEVE: Help her

HAYLEY: Oh fuck off

STEVE: Why not?

HAYLEY: If I go back on, now if I

STEVE: There's no room for

HAYLEY: For what?

STEVE: I don't know

Kindness

Beat.

HAYLEY: Get a job, Steve. Then we'll have a chat about *helping*

STEVE: I've got a job.

HAYLEY: It's not a job, it's an excuse.

Did she tell you what she did? Why I remember her out of the hundreds of lives I've terrorised?

STEVE: You didn't remember her / I had to

HAYLEY: I was drunk, I remembered her in the

Did she tell you what she did?

STEVE: I don't

HAYLEY: She didn't tell you what she did here's what she did

Will you stop doing that while I

STEVE stops spraying.

Big company, kind of place you only know the people on your floor, only those faces and that makes, that can make a company vulnerable that kind of bigness

Means you have to go the extra mile with some things

Security for example

Be extra alert, promote alertness

There'd been thefts a a a *spate* of thefts, computer equipment, hardware going missing and one of the things we

STEVE: She didn't steal anything

HAYLEY looks at STEVE.

What?

HAYLEY: You're very sure of what she is, what she's like

STEVE: Well I

HAYLEY: Are you sure you're not fucking her?

STEVE: I'm not

HAYLEY: You seem to have attached some kind of

STEVE: I'm not fucking her

HAYLEY: She's incredibly important all of a sudden

STEVE: She's got no-one to

HAYLEY: Can I carry on?

> She's coming back into the office one day, been out for lunch and

> Some bloke in some kind of generic IT-support T-shirt's struggling to get through the door with an armful of hard drive

STEVE: Right

HAYLEY: So she helps him

> She holds the door open for him and he smiles and she doesn't check his badge

> She gets back to her desk and there's nothing on it

> *Beat.*

> Y'know, she held open a door for a man stealing *her* computer

> They're supposed to be on *special alert*, she just stands there, holds the door open, lets it happen

STEVE: But anyone could've

HAYLEY: She should have recognised it anyway, covered in stickers apparently, pictures of dogs

STEVE: But everyone

HAYLEY: No, Steve, not everyone. Why is it OK to fuck up like that?

STEVE: It's a big company, *one* computer

HAYLEY: When they're looking to *rationalise* the *headcount* they're going to take stuff like that on b

STEVE: She'd never do it again though, would she? Once you've done something like that

HAYLEY: It's very sad. There it is.

STEVE: It's not just sad it's

Her life is shit

HAYLEY: Really

STEVE: She lives in this basement, crappy little bed-sit

HAYLEY: Bed-sit or studio?

STEVE: Studio whatever it's fucking depressing

HAYLEY: Lots of people / live in

STEVE: D'you know she told me the other day that I am currently the most important person in her life

Me.

Imagine what a shit life that is.

Beat. HAYLEY looks at STEVE. She laughs.

HAYLEY: Poor fucker

STEVE: So I think we should help her.

HAYLEY: She can't go back there, we restructured there's no

STEVE: You could put in a word somewhere

You could call someone

HAYLEY looks away.

Or something

You could do something

Fade.

SCENE 11

GREG's office. Afternoon.

There's a bunch of sunflowers on the desk – still in Interflora wrapping, but the kind of bouquet that stands up by itself, without needing to be transferred into a vase.

GREG is sitting looking through a report, writing notes in the margin with a pencil. HAYLEY comes to the door.

HAYLEY: Hi.

    GREG sits back in his chair and looks at her, then points at the sunflowers.

GREG: From you?

HAYLEY: I thought they looked friendly

GREG: No note.

HAYLEY: It would only have said I'm sorry and I wanted to sa

    To *say* it

    GREG looks at her, waiting.

    I'm sorry.

GREG: From the other side of the fence, are they?

HAYLEY: I'm sorry.

GREG: Do you always say it with metaphorical flowers?

    Did you want to discuss something?

    Beat. HAYLEY takes a deep breath.

HAYLEY: I *am* going to have to stop working on the project

GREG: Right

HAYLEY: As expected

GREG: You don't have a special word for

HAYLEY: What?

GREG: 'Stop working on' it's not very

   Not very *jargon* is it

HAYLEY: I don't

GREG: Don't we have anything to leverage today

HAYLEY: Greg

GREG: No *caveats* to *rationalise* or *incentivise* or

   No *tools* to help us out of this funny

HAYLEY: No

GREG: Everything's a tool, isn't it?

HAYLEY: You're being a bit of a tool, Greg

GREG: You're abandoning my project

HAYLEY: Not abandoning

GREG: Pulling out

HAYLEY: It's in safe hands

GREG: Silly haircuts

HAYLEY: There're reasons

GREG: Personal reasons

HAYLEY: Medical reasons

GREG: Sorry, medical reasons

HAYLEY: You've seen how my hands are

GREG: No proof, have you

HAYLEY: Not that kind of

GREG: My son, he got better soon as I threatened to take his X-Box away

HAYLEY: Now you're just confusing the

GREG: At the end of the day in this day and age you don't have to stop to pull out of a project because of some little thing like your hands don't work

I know a chap steadily losing another ten per cent of his eyesight year on year, can't see a bloody thing now, 'cept blobs and colours and he's working at board level, bright as a button. Someone to do his reading for him, help him up and down stairs but otherwise

So I don't see why you can't get your team of silly haircutted little buggers to do the lifting and carrying for you and let you get on with the thinking bit of the job, the ideas and

HAYLEY: I'm not sure if you realise how debilitating

GREG: I'm sure to you it feels like the whole bloody world's falling apart because you can't pick up your chopsticks, change gear on that natty little car

HAYLEY: It's an automatic

GREG: Still driving?

HAYLEY: Well no, can't grip the wheel

GREG: Looks like the sky is falling down then, doesn't it?

Beat.

If my son got better, pulled himself together or forgot about it or

HAYLEY: Did he go to the doctors?

GREG: Well yes but

HAYLEY: What did they give him?

GREG: Injections

HAYLEY: So he didn't just pull himself together I mean he
    needed something

GREG: You could get injections

HAYLEY: No

GREG: Why not?

HAYLEY: I

    Needles. Don't like them

GREG: How's that going down with the boss?

HAYLEY: I do have the support of the partners they've

GREG: This must affect your prospects, though, mustn't it?

HAYLEY: Please

GREG: As groovy as they try to be, as inclusive and liberal

    Not really going to want a partner with gammy hands are
    they?

    Not very groovy, not very slick

    When you could do something but you won't and you're
    too ill to do your hair neatly

    HAYLEY touches her hair.

    Sorry, too personal?

HAYLEY: They don't

LAURA WADE

GREG: Did it get too personal?

Do they know how personal it got?

Beat.

HAYLEY: Knowing how personal it got, won't it be easier not to have me around?

GREG: I don't know

Woke me up, you did. Almost got me back to the land of the living, bit of an overhaul. Human Performance Review

Brought me out of deep freeze

Sorry if I'm a bit bitter you couldn't

See it through

HAYLEY: I'm sorry, / I didn't

GREG: Are we done?

HAYLEY looks at GREG, then at her lap.

HAYLEY: I need

I need you to sign something

GREG: Do you?

HAYLEY: To say that you're

That you understand the changes to the team working on the project, that I won't be heading it up anymore

GREG: What if I don't sign it?

HAYLEY: There's no reason not to sign it

GREG: Would it piss you off?

HAYLEY: That's not

294

GREG: No, too personal

Beat.

Have a look at it then

HAYLEY: OK

HAYLEY very painstakingly picks up her bag from the floor and tries to slide a piece of paper out of it. GREG watches her. She manages to get the paper out, but it slips from her fingers and floats to the floor.

Just a second

GREG sits back in his chair. HAYLEY bends down and tries to scoop up the piece of paper with both hands. Eventually she gets a grip on it and places it on her side of the desk. GREG looks at her.

GREG: You'll have to pass it to me.

HAYLEY looks at him. She makes a decision.

HAYLEY: Fucker

She bends down to the table and picks up the piece of paper between her teeth. She walks around to GREG's side of the table and places it in front of him, then stands waiting for him to sign.

I trust you've got a pen.

GREG: Yes

GREG takes a pen from his suit pocket and signs the piece of paper. He looks at HAYLEY standing over him.

There. Done.

He stands up, picks up the paper and walks around to HAYLEY's side of the desk. He replaces the paper carefully in her laptop bag and then opens the door for her to leave.

HAYLEY: OK

HAYLEY walks towards her bag to pick it up.

OK

GREG takes the bag and gently places it on HAYLEY's shoulder for her. She tries to smile at him.

Thanks.

I'd shake your hand but

GREG: Yeah.

HAYLEY leaves. GREG sits back down. He looks at the sunflowers. He touches the petals of one of them, gently. He leans in to sniff the flowers, to see if they have a smell. They don't. He sits back in his chair and looks at them.

Fade.

SCENE 12

GREG's office, a couple of weeks later. Afternoon.

There is now a new bunch of Interflora flowers on GREG's desk – not sunflowers this time, but something more romantic. LYDIA stands on GREG's side of the desk, changing the printer cartridge of GREG's printer. GREG stands beside her, a stop-watch in his hand.

LYDIA: Nearly there.

> *LYDIA closes the lid of the printer and sits in GREG's chair. She looks at the screen and clicks the mouse. The printer churns out a page. LYDIA hands it to GREG.*

Test page.

> *GREG stops the stop-watch.*

GREG: Good

> *LYDIA smiles. She gets up out of his chair.*

Pretty good

LYDIA: Bit more difficult with someone timing you

GREG: You didn't panic

> *GREG indicates for LYDIA to sit down opposite him.*

Please

LYDIA: Thank you.

> *GREG looks at LYDIA's CV.*

Nice flowers

GREG: Secret admirer

LYDIA: Lovely

GREG: They're all going mad out there trying to work out who sent them

LYDIA: Office gossip

Your wife or

GREG: Doubt it

GREG looks down at the CV again.

So. Good with computers

LYDIA: Pretty good

GREG: I'm hopeless

Need all the help I can get

LYDIA: I think everyone

Everyone finds it scary

GREG: Yes

LYDIA: Or most people

GREG: Yes

LYDIA: Apart from, you know, actual computer people

GREG: Yes

LYDIA: And even they sometimes don't

GREG: No

LYDIA: And you wonder really, don't you, about taking advice from guys who wear Velcro shoes to work?

GREG laughs.

GREG: Yes

LYDIA: Because you think they can solve everything for you but actually

Beat.

GREG: And other things, what about other things

LYDIA: I'll do anything, I'll make tea

GREG: You wouldn't be opposed

LYDIA: To making tea?

GREG: For a colleague

LYDIA: No, I wouldn't I'd quite like it

To see that someone needed a cup of tea and to make it for them, to identify that need

I mean that's human interaction, isn't it?

GREG: Yes

LYDIA: Just kindness. I do think people should be kinder to people I mean

Not a very trendy thing to say is it, these days

But I'd much rather have a cup of tea made for me by a *person* with a kettle and a tea-bag than just the drinks machine, you know?

Someone who'd noticed I needed one

Beat.

This is a new role, is it?

GREG: Had some consultants in, expecting they'd demand I cull a secretary or two

Not actually *cull*, you know, but

LYDIA: Yes

GREG: Turns out I need *more* people, they reckon a competent Office Manager's just the thing to smooth out the, sorry *optimise efficiency*

Do you say 'schedule' or 'schedule'?

LYDIA: Um, 'schedule's' the English one, isn't it?

GREG: And you say that

LYDIA: Yes

Yes

Or sometimes just 'diary'

GREG: Diary. Like it

Anything you'd like to ask?

LYDIA: Um when will you

GREG: Tomorrow, probably

LYDIA: Well, my number's on my CV so if you need anything else, need to know anything else

LYDIA stands up, shakes GREG's hand confidently and goes to the door. She touches the door handle then turns back.

Um

GREG: Yes?

LYDIA: You should probably know that

Because they'll probably tell you when you call up for references

There was um

It wasn't just overstaffing that got me the redundancy, there was an incident as well

Unfortunately

And you should probably know because it did have some / impact

GREG: I know about the incident, I called them yesterday

You held a door open

LYDIA: Trying to identify a need, I

GREG: Everyone makes mistakes

LYDIA: Yes

GREG: The good people learn

LYDIA: I learned

I really did learn

Thank you.

GREG smiles. LYDIA smiles.

Fade.

SCENE 13

HAYLEY and STEVE's flat. Early evening.

HAYLEY is asleep on the sofa wearing STEVE's pyjamas, her hands folded across her chest like a mummy. STEVE comes in wearing boxer shorts and carrying an empty bin-bag under his arm. He goes to a pile of clothes on the floor and shakes his feet into a pair of jogging pants, then attempts to pull them up using flat hands. HAYLEY wakes up, blinks, looks at STEVE. He sees HAYLEY watching him.

STEVE: Who needs buttons, huh?

HAYLEY smiles.

HAYLEY: Hm

STEVE: You sleep?

HAYLEY: Yeah

STEVE carefully pulls on a T-shirt, again keeping his hands flat, his fingers together. HAYLEY laughs.

STEVE: What?

HAYLEY: Look like a penguin or something

STEVE: Yeah.

STEVE tries to open the bin-bag by blowing on its edge. HAYLEY looks at him.

Thought I'd tidy up a bit

Lydia's coming round

HAYLEY: Is she?

STEVE: Cooking us dinner

HAYLEY: Right

STEVE: Wants to help me look after you

Beat.

Might want to put some clothes on

HAYLEY: Yeah

STEVE: Doesn't matter if you

HAYLEY: No, I will

Look like a

STEVE: She doesn't mind

HAYLEY: Look like a jumble sale

STEVE: You look lovely

HAYLEY: Steve

STEVE: What?

HAYLEY: Don't be sweet I'll cry

STEVE: You alright?

HAYLEY: Want to get better

STEVE: Takes time

HAYLEY: Yeah

STEVE: Think mine might be on the mend

Bit better

HAYLEY: Really?

STEVE: Those injections

HAYLEY looks away.

Sorry

303

HAYLEY: What's dinner?

STEVE: She said maybe stir-fry

HAYLEY looks away.

Oh

HAYLEY: What?

STEVE: Cutlery

HAYLEY: Oh

STEVE: We'll think of something

HAYLEY: Yeah

HAYLEY stands up.

Brush my hair

She looks for her hairbrush.

Where've I put my

It's on the kitchen counter.

Look

Living like a tramp

STEVE has got the bag open and starts to pick up debris from the floor – tissues, food-packaging. HAYLEY picks up the hairbrush and carries it back to the sofa.

STEVE: Not forever, is it?

HAYLEY starts to brush her hair slowly. The movement hurts. STEVE watches. She gets to a knot in her hair which she can't get the brush through. She gives up and throws the brush across the room.

HAYLEY: Fucker.

STEVE: Hey

HAYLEY: Ow

HAYLEY cradles her hand.

STEVE: Hayley

HAYLEY: I just

I can't

STEVE goes to pick up the brush. He looks at her.

I think we're

I can't *do* anything I can't even

STEVE: You started it you did start it

HAYLEY looks at him.

You said you wanted to sleep with someone else

HAYLEY looks away.

HAYLEY: I said I wanted to it didn't mean I would

Didn't mean I was going to

STEVE: Why not?

HAYLEY: Because I didn't really want to, I just wanted you to *mind.*

Beat.

STEVE: I did mind

HAYLEY: You didn't say you minded, you didn't show it or

STEVE hands the brush back to HAYLEY. She looks at him for a long time.

D'you think we can fix this?

Pause. The question hangs in the air.

The doorbell rings.

STEVE: That'll be

HAYLEY: Steve

STEVE: Lydia's here I'll

STEVE goes to answer the door. HAYLEY looks at her hands. LYDIA comes into the room carrying shopping-bags, followed by STEVE. She's wearing smart office clothes.

LYDIA: No I thought of the cutlery problem too but then I was in the Chinese supermarket and they had these

Hi Hayley

HAYLEY: Hi

LYDIA pulls a packet of extra-wide straws out of a shopping-bag.

LYDIA: Look, big straws

Apparently there's some mad Chinese drink with bits in

HAYLEY: Bubble tea

LYDIA: So I thought these'd be perfect so as long I cut things up small you'll be able to suck it up, you'll be able to feed yourselves solid food

Might look a bit silly but

STEVE: No, great

Hayley

HAYLEY: Thank you

LYDIA unpacks the shopping. HAYLEY watches her inhabit the kitchen.

Silence. STEVE looks at HAYLEY.

LYDIA: So anyway the job's fine

STEVE: Sorry. Yeah. Job

LYDIA: Started this morning

STEVE: And?

LYDIA: Great. Knackered

Nice people

HAYLEY: You got a job

LYDIA: Just a boring office job, nothing special. No big deal

LYDIA finishes the unpacking. She puts the empty plastic bags in the bin and looks up to see STEVE and HAYLEY both watching her.

(*To STEVE.*) Dinner'll take like twenty minutes did you want to do the thing first?

STEVE: Yeah

LYDIA: You got them

STEVE: Here

LYDIA: OK

STEVE takes a package from the kitchen and sits on the sofa. HAYLEY moves away.

HAYLEY: Oh god I'm shutting my eyes

LYDIA goes to sit by STEVE on the sofa. During this she opens the package and takes out a syringe.

STEVE: So you like it, you like the people?

LYDIA: New boss took me for a drink this evening, funny chap

HAYLEY stands nervously by the kitchen, her arms around herself.
LYDIA holds the syringe in her hand, gesturing as she talks.

Keeps getting all these flowers delivered to him, and he's a proper bloke, married and everything so the whole office is trying to work out who they're from and either he doesn't know or he's not telling, whole place in a constant state of expectation you can feel it fizzing

Anyway we go for this drink, just me and him and

He tells me just out of the blue he's sent them to himself – like the first bunch was from someone, he wouldn't tell me who, but he liked it so he's been sending them himself, a bunch a week, pretending it's

And now they all think he's fantastic and he's got this new smile because of it so

LYDIA injects STEVE.

And I'm suddenly this person people tell things to I can't imagine why he told me but it makes me

Yeah

LYDIA removes the needle.

Done.

STEVE rubs his hand. He looks at LYDIA. He stands up.

Other one?

STEVE: Hayley

HAYLEY: Yeah

STEVE: There's another shot

HAYLEY shakes her head.

HAYLEY: I can't

Silence.

STEVE and HAYLEY look at each other. STEVE flexes his fingers.

STEVE: Really helps, you know

Once it stops hurting you can actually *think*

LYDIA: Hayley?

HAYLEY: It's needles you know I

STEVE: I'll hold you

I just think we've got to be braver.

HAYLEY comes slowly to the sofa and sits between STEVE's legs. He puts his arms around her waist. LYDIA prepares the shot. HAYLEY screws her face up.

HAYLEY: Aah

STEVE: Brave

HAYLEY: Yeah

HAYLEY holds her hand out for LYDIA to inject and buries her head in STEVE's shoulder. LYDIA injects HAYLEY's hand.

Tss. Ow.

LYDIA: Nearly done

Nearly done

It'll be better before you know it.

Fade.

The end.